# Malta Travel Guide

## Early History and Before History, Tourism Information

Author
Bobby Chapman.

**<u>SONITTEC PUBLISHING</u>**. All rights reserved. No part of this publication may be reproduced, distributed, or transmitted in any form or by any means, including photocopying, recording, or other electronic or mechanical methods, without the prior written permission of the publisher, except in the case of brief quotations embodied in critical reviews and certain other noncommercial uses permitted by copyright law. For permission requests, write to the publisher, addressed “Attention: Permissions Coordinator,” at the address below.

Copyright © 2019 Sonittec Publishing
All Rights Reserved

First Printed: 2019.

**Publisher**:
SONITTEC LTD
College House, 2nd
Floor
17 King Edwards
Road,
Ruislip
London
HA4 7AE

# Table of Content

# Summary

## Travel around the world we live in?

1. (Traveling is easier than you think): We believe that traveling around the world shouldn't be hard: it's actually something everyone should be able to do at least once in their lives. Whether you choose to spend a few years or just a couple months traveling this beautiful planet, it's important to see what's out there. It's up to you to make the dream come true and take the first step. Launch Trip Planner to piece together and price your ideal route. Not sure where to start? You can always call one of our travel consultants and get some complimentary advice!

2.(Travel opens your eyes).: If you're open and willing, travel will make you an incredibly more well-rounded human being. And that's really the goal, isn't it? If you don't know where to start, check out our Around the World planning guide.

3. (Traveling helps you learn who you are).: All the challenges and opportunities travel lays at your feet help you discover who you are in a way that's only possible on the road.

4. (Travel creates meaningful relationships): People you meet while on the road become some of the most valued names on your contact list. They become places on the map to visit later on. These folks give you a glimpse outside your hometown circle of friends, and force you to take in new and refreshing perspectives, and ultimately realize that everyone is the same.

5. (Traveling develops skills you didn't know you had): Sometimes it's only far from home that you realize you you've got skills you've never used. It's travel that brings them to the surface and makes you smile, satisfied to have reached the mountain top, or crossed

a gorge or helped a villager clean up after a storm, or even to have successfully ordered a meal at a rural Chinese restaurant.

6. (Travel helps you learn new languages): There's something satisfying about being able to throw around a few words of Greek, knowing how to say thanks in Thai, pulling out that long dormant Spanish to book a room in Santiago, or simply hearing a language you didn't know existed just a few weeks before.

7. (Travel means adventure): Zip-lining over the jungle canopy in Peru, successfully navigating the maze-like streets of Venice, bartering for the best price in the traditional markets of Marrakech, taking a speedboat ride in New Zealand, or hopping in a Land Rover and heading out to watch animals grazing in Tanzania: these are adventures worth having. People are hardwired for the excitement of adventure and travel may just be the best way to tap into it.

8. (Traveling gives you perspective): Meeting people from other cultures will teach you that the way you've been looking at the world isn't the way everybody else does. In fact, your point-of-view might have some major blind spots. Seeing the world for yourself will improve your vision and your grip on reality.

9. (Travel helps you move forward): If you're between jobs, schools, kids, or relationships, around the world travel can be a perfect way to move from one of these life stages into your next great adventure. A big trip won't just ease your transition into the next stage of your life, it'll give you a chance to reflect on where you've been, where you're going, and where you want to end up.

10. (Travel is education): Seeing the world provides an education that's absolutely impossible get in school. Travel teaches you economy, politics, history, geography, and sociology in an intense, hands-on way no class will. Fortunately, the school of travel is always taking applications, no entrance exam required.

11. (Travel challenges you): Getting your daily latte at the same place and staring at your screen at your nine-to-five every day not nearly interesting enough? Even if you choose to work on the road (and keep staring at the screen), you'll have to find a new place to drink your latte, and depending on your destination, finding coffee, and foamy milk or a good place to sip them could prove to be a sizeable challenge. Travel is full of moments of joy and challenges. Overcoming the challenges gives you some of the greatest joys of all.

12. (Travel shakes things up): It sucks to be stuck in a rut. Everyone knows what that's like. A big trip can be your perfect solution. Fly around the world, stopping over in all of the places you've always wanted to visit. Go ahead and plan your ideal route around the world (it's easier than you think!)

13. (Traveling proves that dreams do come true): You imagined it, daydreamed about it, envisioned it. Guess what? It can be done. Around the world travel is possible, you just have to decide you're willing to take

the first step and start planning your itinerary. What are you waiting for? We've put together some specials to inspire you to live your dream.

14. (Travel gives you cool stories): Let's face it. Even for folks who can't tell a story, just the words "last year in Mongolia" get you instant party points. Even when events seem trivial, nostalgia and distance create an irresistible spin that makes mundane things like getting your laundry done in Zanzibar, entertaining. Just don't be that person and overdo it!

15. (Travel is literally food for thought).: You'll be constantly surprised at the flavors the world has to offer. The way people in other cultures and countries prepare food, and break bread together (not that all cultures even eat bread) will astound you.

16. (Travel gives you a sense of accomplishment): If you're the kind of person that dreams big, you're probably one to reach for new challenges. Finishing a trip gives you the satisfaction that you were able make

a goal to travel and accomplish what you set out to do see the world.

17. (Traveling for the hell of it): Why travel? Because you can. Because you want to. Because it beats the alternative (staying home). Why not pick up your tickets and get the ball rolling!

# Malta History

## Introduction

The Maltese Islands - Malta, Gozo and Comino - lie in the narrow channel joining the eastern and western basins of the Mediterranean, sixty miles south of Sicily and 180 miles north of Tunisia. The islands occupy an area of just 122 square miles.

Malta, the larger island, has a number of natural harbours which have given the island strategic importance in the Mediterranean. In effect, the power controlling Malta has always been in a position to influence events in the Mediterranean.

For this reason, the islands were occupied by the Phoenicians, the Romans, the Byzantines, the Arabs, the Normans, the Swabians, the Angevins, the Aragonese, the Castillians, the Order of St. John, the French and the British. In 1964 Malta finally gained its Independence.

Not much is known about Malta's prehistoric inhabitants except that they came from the north and found Malta suitable to build great megalithic temples. They hollowed huge hypogea (underground temples) out of Malta's soft rock and developed an art and sculpture unequalled in Western Europe in their time and for many centuries later.

The presence of the Phoenicians and Carthaginians in Malta opened the islands to widespread trade which increased under the Romans, who established flourishing communities in Malta, building sophisticated complexes and bringing their culture and prosperity to the islands.

Malta was conquered by Muslims in 870 AD after three centuries of Byzantine rule. After a period of desolation, the ancient city of Mdina was rebuilt in the 11th century. Not much remains of this period other than Malta's Semitic language.

After changing hands many times, in 1530 the Order of the Knights of St John arrived in Malta and in 1565 Malta was besieged for three months by a Turkish armada in what has become famously known as the Great Siege of Malta. The Order's victory marked a turning point in Turkish expansion in Europe and the Mediterranean. Indeed, the hard-fought and bloody victory made the Order and Malta famous throughout Europe.

Realising that they had to make the island safe from future attacks, the Knights decided to build a fortress city on the peninsula overlooking Malta's Grand Harbour. The city was named Valletta after the ruling Grand Master, Jean Parisot de Valette - the victor of the Great Siege of 1565 - and became Malta's capital city in 1566. Today, it is renowned for its Baroque palaces and churches.

After the Siege, Malta started its second golden age. During the 17th and 18th centuries, the island's population flourished. Towns and villages grew and were enriched by villas, palaces and churches. A highly successful merchant class traded far and wide and the arts flourished in the homes of the rich and the churches. This age was brought to a sudden end by the anti-aristocratic French Revolution which seized the Order’s properties in France, limiting its funds and its function. The final blow came on 13 June 1798 when Napoleon Bonaparte made Malta French.

Eventually, angered by the brutality and looting of the French Revolutionary soldiers, the Maltese could not accept the radical reforms "to liberate the people from feudalism" imposed by the new rulers. Revolt broke out within three months, forcing the French forces to retreat behind the massive fortifications of Valletta and the three harbour cities of Cospicua,Vittoriosa and Senglea. The Maltese leaders of the Revolt called on their lawful king, Ferdinand, King of the Two Siciliesas

Charles V's successor, to help them drive out the occupying French. Ferdinand requested the British Admiral in the Mediterranean, Horatio Nelson, to help his loyal subjects, leading to a two-year land and sea blockade of Valletta and the harbour cities in which many Maltese died.

British diplomacy and dubious dealings led some of the leaders of the Revolt to ask for British Protection, which was quickly accepted in 1802. Twelve years later, the Treaty of Paris, legalised Britain's possession of Malta and for the next 150 years, Malta was Britain's colony in the Mediterranean, and the base for its mighty Mediterranean Fleet together with a large garrison (troops of soldiers).

To the disappointment of the Maltese, the British imposed an autocratic regime with a British governor at its head. The Maltese soon embarked on a political struggle for autonomy, an unequal struggle marked by imprisonments, deportations and repeated suspension of democratic government which was eventually granted in 1921.

The military character of the island became stronger in times of war. During World War I, Malta acted as 'The Nurse of the Mediterranean', receiving thousands of wounded soldiers, especially from the failed Gallipoli campaign. In World War IIMalta was in the centre of the battle for the control of the Mediterranean between the Italian and German forces in Italy and North Africa and the British 8th Army supported by Malta. The island received the heaviest concentrations of bombing of all Europe, suffering starvation and heavy military and civilian deaths. However its brave resistance was recognised by the award of the George Cross; the highest civilian medal. Once again, the islands' resistance proved to be the turning point of a European war.

In 1964, Malta became a sovereign independent state strengthened by an industrial background based on the shipyards and a strong educational, health and administrative structure. British influence, culture and the war had completely changed Malta and the Maltese. English had replaced Italian as the language of culture, with Maltese becoming the national language of the reborn Island State which became a Republic in 1974. In May 2004, Malta became a member of the European Union, and in January 2008 a member of the Euro zone.

# Malta before History

In the Genesis, the first book of the Bible, we read:

God also said: Let the waters that are under the heaven be gathered together into one place; and let the dry land appear. And it was done. And God called the dry land Earth; and the gathering together of the waters, he called Seas. And God saw that it was good.

Before land there was the water. The science of plate tectonics and continental drift tells us that the earth's land masses are always moving and clashing, as are the oceans. Our planet is alive and in constant motion.

Many millions of years ago, all the present continents were one land mass – called *Pangea* – surrounded by an ocean known as *Panthalassa*.

About 200 million years ago, this super-continent split into two land masses: Laurasia in the north and Gondwana in the south, with an ocean in between. That ocean is known as the Sea of Tethys.

Fast forward by one hundred million years to when these two enormous land masses also started breaking up and drifting, slowly creating the world as we know it today. This was not a smooth or speedy process: the tectonic plates broke up and collided again and again, something they are still doing today. We know that the part of the African plate carrying Algeria and Morocco is slowly moving towards Spain, that Tunisia and Libya are drifting towards Sicily (with Malta in the way) and that Italy is moving east. To compensate, the Greek plate is moving west as is Turkey. In millions of years from now, the Mediterranean may look very different from how it is today.

Back to Tethys. Originally this sea simply divided the two land masses of Laurasia and Gondwana which together made up all the land on this planet. But when the two masses started moving and breaking up, the Sea of Tethys had to do so too. At the same time, other mini-plates split, grouped and regrouped. When the Middle East joined up to Turkey, the large Sea of Tethys was divided, creating the Mediterranean Sea as we know it.

The present Mediterranean is 3,800 km long with an average width of about 1,000 km. It is divided into two large basins, evidence of its changing past. The Tyrrhenian Sea between Italy and Sardinia is 3600 metres deep, while the much larger eastern basin reaches a depth of 4,000 metres. The process of its creation also divided the central part into other mini-seas like the Ligurian, the Tyrrhenian, the Adriatic, the Ionian and the Aegean.

There is a reason for this. Recent surprising discoveries show that the Mediterranean actually dried out and was refilled several times in its history. By studying the ocean floor, scientists could conclude that the connection with the Atlantic at the Straits of Gibraltar had been blocked more than once. The inflow of water from the rivers running into the Mediterranean was not enough to make up for the loss of water by evaporation. These phases of drying out, together with the climatic changes that led to various Ice Ages, caused major drops in the sea level and allowed dry land to appear and reconnect Africa and Europe more than once, dividing the sea into a series of lakes. Flora and fauna started travelling along the land-bridges while marine life began developing separately.

Scientists have come across remains of sunken sites which showed that for some time, they had emerged from the water and subsequently submerged again. In Israel, a string of underwater Neolithic villages has been discovered, complete with typical Stone Age houses, about 200 metres from the shore. A collection of flint tools some 45,000 years old was discovered on the continental shelf off the island of Corfu. Other remains have been found near Nice in France and off the Aegean islands of Milos and Agios Petros.

All this shows that early humans spread around and across the Mediterranean in all directions. During the Palaeolithic Age, they started to use fire and bury the dead. They may also have been visiting reachable islands in primitive boats and occasionally settling there. Eventually modern humans developed art and agriculture. The Neolithic period has provided plenty of evidence regarding the first permanent settlements, the use of pottery, the domestication of animals and the beginning of religious beliefs.

And this brings us to Malta. As a result of the agriculture revolution, the establishment of commercial networks and improvements in boat-building, the smaller islands became attractive for permanent settlement. Malta's pre-history does not start with Għar Dalam, but with the evolution of the sea and land around our island home. The evolution of

Mediterranean humans has been tightly bound up with the sea around us. It still is and therefore we need to understand its changes and the dangers of pollution and over-fishing.

The main challenge now is the preservation and renewal of the Mediterranean and its common culture, where a great civilisation began. For many thousands of years, this once great sea has provided both a barrier and a bridge for the people who live around it. While political, religious and racial developments still divide us, there seems to be a general coming together to tackle problems that no one nation can solve on its own.

## The Period of Romans

It appears that the first recorded contact of the Maltese Islands with the Romans took place in 255BC, during the First Punic War. The Roman fleet was on its way back from an expedition to Africa when they stopped in Malta, pillaged whatever they could carry away and set alight the rest. Clearly, at the time, the Romans did not recognize the strategic significance of the islands.

However, the Carthaginians who ruled Malta in that period, presumed that sooner or later the Romans would return to take over the islands. Therefore, they took some military measures in order to avoid invasion and in 218BC, when the Romans came back, they had a Carthaginian garrison of almost 2,000 men under the command of Hamilcar. Yet this tactic served for nothing as apparently, the Romans did not even have to fight in order to take over Malta in that year.

From 218BC, Malta was included in the newly formed province of Sicily and for many centuries, these islands shared the same faith. It is not known what part Malta played in the civil wars that brought about the collapse of the Republic constitution in Rome in 27BC. Most probably, Malta was not involved since Cicero, the great orator, was at one point considering going into voluntary exile on the island.

Once under their rule, initially, the Romans did not impose themselves on the Maltese people. In fact, from the material evidence available, one can observe that the islands retained Punic artistic fashions and that the Punic language was still spoken, though not written, on official documents till the 1st century AD and probably longer.

Three different cultures and languages met in Malta. Though retaining Punic culture, the Roman administration introduced Latin (at least for official work), and its own cultural fashions. Alongside these two cultures there was the Greek one which had already spread in the Punic world and became stronger with the growth of Rome.

Meanwhile, Roman occupation introduced also new reforms in governance and religion. This development is evident in the coinage of the islands as they change their imagery and language more or less in this order: Egyptian religious imagery, Punic language, Punic divine iconography, Greek language, Hellenized divine iconography, and ultimately, Roman images and Latin language.

As subjects controlled by Rome, the Maltese people enjoyed no special privileges and were subject to an established taxation system. For a time, the islands were granted the right to govern themselves and were even allowed their own representation at Rome. However, this all changed in 27BC with the reorganization of the Roman empire and the introduction of the imperial age by its first emperor Augustus. Consequently, like many other Sicilian cities, Malta and Gozo lost their local self-government and the right to issue their own money.

Christianity was introduced to the islands in 60AD, when on his way to face trial in Rome, St Paul was shipwrecked in Malta. Yet contrarily to the general belief that the locals turned into Christians, material evidence indicates that the religion practiced officially on both islands from the 1st down to the 3rd century was the Roman pagan one, with a high dose of imperial worship. Till now, there is no archaeological record which confirms the practice of Christianity at this time, though some people might have followed this new religion clandestinely without leaving a trace.

Deep political, economic and spiritual crisis affected the Roman empire between the 4th and 3rd centuries AD. This eventually led to its division during the reign of Constantine I, when the seat of power was moved to Byzantium, thereby renaming the city Constantinople and creating the Roman empire of the east or the Byzantine empire.

Although Malta was under Byzantine rule for four centuries, not much is known about this period other than that Germanic tribes, including the Vandals and Ostrogoths, briefly took control of the islands before the Byzantines launched a counter-attack and reclaimed them.

It is during the reign of Justinian, in 535AD, that the Maltese Islands were assimilated within the Byzantine empire, along with Sicily. They remained part of it until they were won over by the Muslim Arabs in 870AD.

# The Arab Period

## Arab rule in Malta

For reasons that have deep religious and cultural roots, it must be admitted that many Maltese people find it difficult to accept their Arab and Muslim past. Yet the very language that is spoken in Malta is basically a Semitic language with main words, like all the numbers and the names of basic foods, being perfectly recognizable by Arab speakers. Even the grammar has strong Arab roots and likewise several place names all over the islands.

Malta was conquered by Muslims in 870 AD after three centuries of Byzantine rule. The effects of that conquest caused ripples across the centuries that can be felt up to the present day. Various Muslim sources but no Byzantine ones record the conquest of Malta.

This reminds one of the saying that history is writter by the victors.

After Muhammad's death in 632 AD, Islam spread across the whole of the Middle East and North Africa including parts of southern Europe such as Sicily, Spain and Malta. Some historians claim that among the general looting, some Christian structures in Malta were dismantled and taken to Sousse, in present day Tunisia, as a prestigious reminder of their conquest.

Although Muslim sources do not spell it out, it is reasonable to assume that the Muslim victors dealt merciless with the defeated. This is because the only report that speaks of the years immediately after 870 AD mentions an 'uninhabited ruin' when speaking of Malta. In fact no archaeological remains were ever found from the years immediately after 870 AD, while $10^{th}$ and $11^{th}$ century pottery, typically Arab, was unearthed at Mesquita square, Mdina.

ounding of the city of al-Mahdiyya in ,nt a new development for Malta, as ships sa. n Sicily to this new capital had to cross very close to the Maltese islands. This placed Malta at the centre of an important political and commercial route. However this was a dangerous route due to the risk of pirates and this meant that the Muslim conquerors had to keep a number of soldiers on the Maltese islands in order to protect this sea route.

Al-Himyari who recorded the events of that period says of Malta "The Island was visited by shipbuilders because the wood in it is of the strongest kind, by fishermen because of the abundance and tastiness of the fish around its shores, and by those who collect honey because that is the most common thing there."

The mid 11th century marks the arrival of many new settlers and the rebuilding of Malta's ancient capital city Mdina. Many finds of 11th century ceramics confirm that by this time a growing community existed in Mdina. The ceramics are similar to ones found in

Sicily indicating trade between the two regions. Similar finds in the Gozo Citadel confirm the same for the sister island. Moreover there is evidence of the importation of food, and this would only have become necessary by the presence of a large population.

Between 1048-49, Malta was attacked by the Byzantines who tried to reconquer the islands. The Muslims came together and when they counted themselves, they found that their slaves outnumbered the free men. So they offered freedom to their slaves in return for helping them to drive back the attackers. They succeeded in this and the islands were not attacked again. However one must be careful when dealing with records by writers of the period who may have been influenced one way or another.What really happened is uncertain, as in countless other ages, 'history' could have been written by biased observers.

What is clear from the above account is that the local community was composed of masters and slaves. It is unclear whether the slaves were all Christians and whether Malta was their place of origin or the place that they were brought to after capture. Because many village names such as Farruġ, Ġawhar, Kbir and Safi started off in this period, it is plausible to assume that the first *'raħal'* settlements also originate from this time.

Around 1091, Count Roger of Normandy landed in Malta defeating the Muslim resistance, which soon surrendered and agreed: to recognize him as the overlord, to give up their weapons, to pay an annual sum, and to release their Christian captives. The Christian captives came out of 'il-Medina' tearful with joy at their sudden liberation and welcomed Count Roger's rule with shouts of *"Kyrie eleyson"* (Greek for "Lord have mercy on us").

Yet in reality, contrary to legend, Count Roger's visit did not mark the end of Muslim presence in Malta, as it was not much more than a raid to control Malta before taking over Tunis and North Africa. In fact, it was in 1127 when Count Roger's son, King Roger, took over the island when it was threatened by a Muslim rebellion, that Europeanisation started. Still, Islamcontinued in Malta for over a century and long after 1127; the official languages of Malta and Sicily were probably, Latin, Classical Arabic and Greek.

Christianity was reintroduced in Malta by King Roger in 1127 and flourished there ever since. At first, Greek Byzantine influence was supreme, but the Latin (Western) Church favoured by the Normans eventually took over in Malta.

# Medieval Malta

At the end of the tenth century the centre of the Mediterranean was a battlefield for the three great powers of the time: the Byzantines, the Muslims and the Normans. The Normans first arrived in Italy in 1014AD and by the middle of the eleventh Century their leader, Roger Hauteville became a powerful Count in Italy. By 1091 the Normans took over all ofSicily from the Arabs after thirty years of on-going warfare. From there Count Roger sailed to Malta.

The Arab rulers in Malta quickly surrendered to the Normans and the terms of surrender included that all Christian slaves be freed. All horses and weapons were to be turned over to the Normans and freedom of worship was allowed for all, with Christians and Moslems being treated equally. However, the image of religious tolerance or equality must be questioned as after all non-Christians were required to pay a tax. At this time many churches and chapels were rebuilt. The legend that Malta's national flag originates from Count Roger's coat of arms is a recent myth, but this story is still so strong that Masses are said on the 4th of November for the repose of the Count's soul.

A historian of that time, Idrisi, described Malta as 'A large island with a safe harbour which opens to the East. Malta has a city and it abounds in grazing land, flocks, fruit and, above all, honey.' Place names from that period are often made up of Arab words like 'mrieħel' (flocks), variations of 'ġnien' (garden) and 'mġiebaħ' (apiaries). Amongst many others.

Until 1156 the Archbishop of Palermo was in charge of the Maltese diocese but in 1168 the bishop of Malta, John, is mentioned by name. However, a Muslim tombstone found in Gozo records the death of Maimuna, a Moslem girl, on Thursday 21 March 1174. Therefore the religions existed side by side for a long time after Count Roger's son King Roger took over Malta fully in 1127. By the end of the 12th Century the Norman reign in Southern Italy, Sicily and Malta (which was often treated as an extension of Sicily) had crumbled for several reasons including attacks by naval forces from Pisa and Genoa.

In 1250 Pope Clement IV invited Charles of Anjou and Provence to take over Sicily. This created disputes and battles raged for 18 years. Charles was victorious but he was a tyrant and his Angevin dynasty was short-lived. An uprising began at the start of Vespers in Sicily, the sunset prayer marking the beginning of the night vigil on Easter Monday, March 30, 1282. These uprising became known and termed as the "Sicilian Vespers". Within six weeks, the Sicilian rebels killed 3,000 French men and women and the government of King Charles lost control of the island. Although his rule was quite just, unrest was simmering in Sicily because the island played a subordinate role in Charles's empire.In 1282 the Aragonese fleet in Sicily greeted Peter III of Aragon with great joy. He was crowned king of Sicily in 1283. Later that year, the Battle of Malta took place on July 8, 1283, at the entrance to the Grand Harbour, as the Aragonese fleet appeared. The Grand Harbour was to witness the first major battle to be fought in its vicinity. The Angevin fleet was defeated, much to the joy of the Maltese as like their fellow Sicilians, had rose against the Angevins. This meant that the rule of the Aragonese begun in the Maltese islands. Although the Angevin rule over Malta was short, it was during this period that Malta mostly began to be absorbed into the Latin and European systems of laws and government.

During the Aragonese period, Malta, although officially part of the kingdom of Sicily was often given as a 'fiefdom' to a nobleman who then became 'Count of Malta'. Hence in the period between 1283 and 1350, the kings of Aragon granted political authority including taxing to a succession of Sicilians awarding them the titles of marquis or count of Malta.

In 1350 the Maltese begged King John I of Aragon for Malta and Gozo to cease the direct rule from Sicily and to place the island under his own domain. In fact an agreement was signed that same year. However, subsequent kings ignored this agreement and it was only after widespread discontent between 1393 and 1397 that once again led King Martin I in 1398 re-ordered that the Maltese islands were not to be given as a fief.

This promise was broken once again in 1420 under the rule of Aragonese King Alfonso V. A new feudal lord made the Maltese pay heavy taxes and by 1425 under yet another count, Gonsalvo Monroi (or Monroy), the

Maltese were reduced to poverty. The situation was so miserable that the Maltese offered to pay Monroi the sum of 30,000 florins that he had paid for the islands. In January 1427 the Maltese obtained what they wanted and moreover, Mdina was granted the title of 'Citta Notabile'. As a result a Maltese self-government known as the *Universita'* was formed. The repayment of all that money was not an easy task for Malta and to make matters worse Malta was invaded by pirates and then ravaged by a plague from 1427 to 1428.

After the death of King Alfonso V and then of his brother, the Maltese Islands passed under joint Sicilian and Spanish rule as Spain ruled over Sicily. Under the new King Ferdinand and Queen Isabella there was more misery in store for the Maltese when a huge army of 18,000 men from Tunisia attacked Malta and Gozo. The total Maltese population at the time was slightly less than the attacking forces so although they tried to resist they failed and some 3,000 Maltese were dragged away to slavery.

Following this disaster King Ferdinand ordered the building of Fort St Elmo, actually not much more than a tower, at the mouth of the Grand Harbour. This was the same fort that was later enlarged by the Knights and played an enormous part in the defense of Malta in the 1565 siege.

In 1522 the Knights of the Order of St John of Jerusalem were driven out of Rhodes by the Turks and after wandering Europe for a period of 8 years, King Charles V of Spain gave Malta to the Knights as a base. This marks the end of Malta's Medieval period as Malta's stormy and feudal history from the eleventh to the fifteenth century meant that socially, Malta did not benefit much from the social and artistic Renaissance of the rest of Europe.

# The Knights Hospitallers and Malta

The loss of Rhodes to the Ottoman Turks in 1523 caused the Hospitaller Order of St John to become dependent upon the Emperor Charles V for a new role and home. The Emperor, facing an Ottoman threat to Vienna in the East and the capture of Algiers by Barbarossa in the south, needed a barrier against the invasion of Italy and Spain. Charles thus offered Malta and Tripoli to the Order for the annual rent of a (Maltese) falcon. Due to internal disagreements created by the enmity between France and Spain, which influenced the Hospitallers, six years passed before they finally accepted the Emperor's offer and took possession of the Maltese islands in November 1530.

The islands' population was then around 12,000. Expecting an attack from the Ottoman Empire, the Order of St John transferred the centre of Government from Notabile (Mdina) to Birgu in view of its strategic harbour location.

Under the guidance of Grand Masters L`Isle Adam, de Homedes, and de Valette, the Knights fortified the Grand Harbour by constructing Fort St Elmo on the tip of Mount Sciberras, strengthened the walls of the medieval *Castello a Mare* (later St Angelo) at Birgu, deepening and widening the ditch separating it from Birgu. The Knights purchased a large chain from Venice to protect the Order's galleys within the creek between Birgu and *L'Isola*, on which was built Fort St Michael.

In 1551, Barbarossa's successor, Dragut, launched an attack on Malta, which failed, however he succeeded in carrying off almost the entire population of Gozo as slaves, and also in capturing Tripoli.

These events led up to the much larger attack by Suleiman's army and navy on Malta in 1565, which came to be known as the Great Siege. In April of that year, an estimated 40,000 men on 180 galleys left Constantinople and sailed for Malta, arriving on 18th May. The Order had at its disposal around 540 Knights and sergeants at arms, 400 Spanish troops sent by Don Garcia de Toledo, Viceroy of Sicily (including his own son Fadrique, who was to die defending Malta) and some 4000 Maltese militia. A further 500 Spanish troops came to Malta's defence at a later stage.

The Ottoman (Turkish) army was commanded by Mustapha Pasha, and the fleet by Suleiman's son-in-law, Piali Pasha. Dragut arrived 2 weeks later with more troops and artillery. The Ottomans, with such a long line of communications, knew they had to conquer before the winter; they attacked Fort St Elmo on 25th May, committing the feared 6000 Janissaries to the battle, confidently expecting victory in a week; in the event, it took until 23rd June, with the loss of 8000 troops, including Dragut, to overwhelm the Fort. The rest of the summer was dominated by continuous assaults on Birgu and L'Isla; the latter was on the verge of falling on 7th August, but a false rumour of an assault on the Ottoman camp in Marsa led to a retreat at the last moment.

As the bloodiest siege that Europe had ever seen waged through summer, Don Garcia persuaded Catholic Europe to gather a relief force for Malta; an army of 10,000 landed on the island on 6th September, destroyed the most of the rear of the Ottoman forces on the 7th, and chased them to the sea by the 8th. The Siege was over.

In order to safeguard Malta against any future invasions, de Valette immediately began to build a fortified city on the strategically important Mount Sciberras, later to called Valletta. The Hospitallers (subsequently known as the Knights of Malta) gained legendary status in Christian Europe following the events of 1565 and the subsequent involvement of the Order's galleys alongside the Venetian fleet in the destruction of the Ottoman fleet at Lepanto in 1571. The Order's coffers, filled with donations from its European admirers, lined the island with watchtowers and completed the reconstruction of the damaged forts around Valletta. Grand Masters were raised to the status of Prince by the European powers, and that of Cardinal by the Catholic Church.

In addition, the Hospitaller Order became renowned for the teaching and practice of medicine in Europe;

the Sacra Infirmeria was able to accommodate 500 patients and included a medical and pharmacy school.

Although always dependent upon Europe for provisions, Malta flourished culturally and socially between the 16th and 18th centuries; the Co-Cathedral of St John the Baptist in Valletta became an architectural and artistic jewel; palaces, University and a school of Mathematics and Nautical Sciences and a public library were established.

Militarily, the Order attained its height of strength during the 17th century, its galleys crossing the central Mediterranean, fighting and capturing Barbary corsair galleys, but also European vessels, leading to periods of tension.

By the end of the 18th century, the Order had declined in influence; lack of discipline undermined its success; funding declined, as did its role in Europe.

On 9th June 1798, on his way to Egypt, Napoleon Bonaparte attacked Malta. Deprived of the protection of the defeated King of Naples and Sicily and weakened by divided loyalties amongst the Spanish and French Knights, the Order meekly surrendered on 12th June after brief resistance put up by Maltese militias.

So ended the Order of Malta's rule over the island. Unusually among Grand Masters, Hompesch resigned, leaving a broken Order to rediscover itself gradually over the following 25 years; it settled, first in Sicily, and, subsequently in Rome, where it remains today, recognised as a sovereign government, with its Grand Magistry located in the Via Condotti. The Order has been granted a 99 year lease on Fort St Angelo and is engaged in restoration work on this historic structure.

## The French Occupation

On the 9 June 1798, a French fleet destined for Egypt with over 30,000 men under General Napoleon Bonaparte arrived off the heavily fortified citadel of Valletta, ruled by the Knights of St John. A French Knight in Malta recorded the event in these terms: "the

Maltese people saw from vantage points, the forest of masts which covered a vast expanse of sea....the sight petrified us."

Grand Master Ferdinand von Hompesch refused Bonaparte's demand that his convoy would be allowed to enter Valletta and take on supplies, insisting that only two ships could enter at a time, upon which Bonaparte immediately ordered his fleet to bombard Valletta and landed several thousand soldiers at seven strategic sites around the island.

Most French knights commanding various strategic localities and forts deserted the Order. However, many Maltese regiments offered brave resistance in spite of the confusion. At Fort Tigne, the Maltese *Cacciatori* regiment threw back three times the attacking French forces. In Fort San Lucian at Marsaxlokk, the Maltese garrison put up a fierce resistance for 36 hours and the 165 men only gave up when they ran out of water and ammunition.

The demoralized Order however failed to mount a strong resistance and once the city of Mdina fell to Bonaparte, Hompesch surrendered Malta and all its resources to the French, in exchange for estates and pensions in France for himself and his knights.

Napoleon stayed in Malta for a few days during which time his troops established an administration controlled by his officers: introducing radical changes to limit the influence of the Bishop to purely religious matters, expelling all foreign clergy, and passing laws defending the rights of illegitimate children. The education system was reformed to focus on scientific subjects and a civil code was drawn up introducing equality before the law, freedom of religion and property rights. Slavery was abolished and all Turkish slaves were freed. All aristocratic rights and privileges were abolished.

He then sailed for Egypt, leaving behind 4,000 soldiers who were deeply unpopular with the Maltese due to their hostility towards Catholicism. During the short period of French rule, Mdina and its nobles played a great part in the rising of the Maltese against their French rulers. At that time the Maltese were extremely loyal to their religious leaders and their faith,and resistant to liberal ideas.

When the French began meddling with their churches and looting them of their silver, matters came to a head. The last straw came when, on September 2nd, the French ordered the auctioning of the damask of the Carmelite Church. This was opposed by an angry crowd and rioting broke out. A French officer by the name of Masson was attacked and thrown from a balcony in nearby Rabat, dying on the spot along with some of his men. Meanwhile, Col. Masson's wife was only spared because she was expecting a child. The French troops took refuge behind the walls of Malta's fortified cities, where they were blockaded by the Maltese militia.

When the French Mediterranean Fleet was destroyed at the Battle of the Nile on 1 August 1798, the British

Royal Navy was able to start a blockade of Malta, assisted by the Maltese rebellion against French rule. Forced to retreat to Valletta, the French troops faced such food shortages, that they were reduced to eating cats and rats. Although small quantities of supplies arrived in early 1799, starvation and disease had a disastrous effect on the health and morale of the French troops.

The Kingdom of Naples and Sicily along with Great Britain sent ammunition and aid to the Maltese and blockaded the islands, stopping French convoys to and from Malta, forcing them to surrender to larger British squadrons in hard-fought battles. These defeats weakened so much the French position in Valletta that after a two-year siege, General Belgrand de Vaubois surrendered his garrison, exhausted by malnutrition and typhus disease, on the 4th of September 1800.

Maltese leaders presented their islands to Sir Alexander Ball asking that the island become a British Dominion. The Maltese people created a Declaration of

Rights in which they agreed to come "under the protection and sovereignty of the King of the free people, His Majesty the King of the United Kingdom of Great Britain and Ireland". The Declaration also stated that "his Majesty has no right to cede these Islands to any power...if he chooses to withdraw his protection, and abandon his sovereignty, the right of electing another sovereign, or of the governing of these Islands, belongs to us, the Maltese alone, and without control".

Malta was retained by Britain, and control of the island was a reason for the outbreak of the Napoleonic Wars in 1803. Ultimately it remained under British government for 164 years, gaining Independence in 1964.

## British Rule in Malta

Of all the periods in Maltese history, the time when Malta was a British colony is the one that still generates emotional debate. The main reason for this is that many Maltese still remember British rule with a certain degree of nostalgia. Likewise, British nationals presently residing in Malta always point out that the British were *invited* to Malta.

In the first months after the insurrection against the French, the Maltese leaders realised that they needed a great power to help them expel the French and protect their national sovereignty. First, they appealed to the King of Naples for help but having trouble with Napoelon himself, help instead came from the British who were allies with Naples and rivals of the French at that time.

In February 1799 Captain Alexander Ball was appointed president of the National Congress. In March 1799 the Congress petitioned King Ferdinand IV of Naples to transfer his sovereign rights to King George III of Great Britain. King George accepted the Maltese demand and granted the Maltese 'nation' full protection and the enjoyment of all their dearest rights. In October 1801 the Congress declared not to surrender the islands to any other power except Britain, nor would they accept back the Order of St. John. The British were here to stay and by 1813 Malta was declared a Crown colony. However, Maltese patriots felt cheated because they wanted Malta to be ruled by a Maltese elected assembly and the role of the British would have been only that of protectors of the islands.

Although the British brought improvements to the Maltese economy, education and medical sectors,the Maltese longed for self rule. They never forgot that they had *asked* the British to come to Malta to expel the French. As soon as World War I ended the Maltese petitioned the British for self-government. On 1 November 1921 a joyful populace attended the opening ceremony of the first Maltese Parliament by the Prince of Wales. At that time, Italian was the language of the Church, of the law and of 'society'. Because of this the question of English or Italian being taught in schools created a difficult problem in Parliament. This problem combined with issues regarding the Governor's powers resulted in the constitution being revoked. In 1939 a constitution allowing for a parliament with a minority of Maltese citizens was granted, but the beginning of World War II caused local government to be suspended.

During the first years of British rule the island was not given much importance but its excellent harbours became a prized asset especially after the opening of the Suez Canal. The island went on to become a military and naval fortress, the headquarters of the British Mediterranean fleet. During the Great War (World War I), Malta came to be known as thenurse of the Mediterranean as it served as a hospital for the injured. Meanwhile, its strategic position led to its own drawback during WW II when the island suffered heavy bombing and many casualties. It was during this period, in 1942, that the George Cross was awarded and it to this day forms part of the Maltese flag: "To honour her brave people I award the George Cross to the island fortress of Malta to bear witness to a heroism and devotion that will long be famous in history".

After World War II the islands achieved self-rule once again and then the question of whether Malta should be integrated with Britain or achieve independence was one that would occupy the Maltese for over a decade. Independence was granted in 1964 but Malta was still considered a Monarchy under Queen Elizabeth II. By 1974 Malta became a Republic with the head of state being a Maltese President. The decreasing strategic importance of Malta to the Royal Navy meant that the British government was increasingly reluctant to maintain the naval dockyards and by 1979 Malta stopped being used as a British military base.

To this day the presence of the British influence in Malta is felt throughout the islands, from the use of English as one of Malta's official languages to the many buildings and monuments. The British introduced the Neoclassical style of architecture to Malta, evident in several palaces built during this period, in the Greek revival portico of the parish church of Sta. Marija Assunta in Mosta, and in the soaring spire of St Paul's Anglican Cathedral which dominates the Valletta skyline. Neo-Gothic architecture was also introduced to Malta during this period, in the Chapel of Santa Maria Addolorata at Malta's main cemetery, and in the Carmelite Church in Sliema. Sliema itself, which developed from a sleepy fishing village into a bustling, cosmopolitan town during the British period, once boasted an elegant seafront that was famed for its Regency style architecture, strongly reminiscent of the British seaside town of Brighton.

# War Period and History

## Malta at War I

### Conscription, Rationing and the Mediterranean Campaigns

This series of articles commemorating the 70th anniversary of Malta's role World War II recalls the situation after the end of the blitz on HMS Illustrious in

January 1941 and the heavy Luftwaffe attacks on the island which continued until May of that year, the introduction of rationing, conscription and the war in the Mediterranean.

The German air raids on Malta were on a much larger scale than those carried by the Regia Aeronautica between June 11 and December 1940. The highest number of air raid alerts, 107, was in February 1941; there were 105 in March, 92 in April and 98 in May.

In February 1941, the government decided to introduce general rationing. The system adopted was already in force in the north of Malta under the Marquis Barbaro of St George, who had devised the system and who was appointed Food Distribution Officer.

The first commodities rationed were sugar, matches, soap and coffee, and the scheme came into force on April 7, 1941. Later, other items, such as cigarettes, were rationed too.

Laurence Mizzi has written several books on wartime reminiscences by people who suffered hardship and deprivation, as did the rest of the population, because of lack of foodstuffs, which forced the authorities to introduce rations.

Dolores Penza's family had to leave Cospicua, one of the Three Cities which bore the brunt of enemy air raids, and went to live in Luqa. Her husband was a head-teacher, so when he arrived at Luqa he took charge of the local primary school. He was also Luqa Protection Officer:

"One of my husband's jobs was to organise the rationing and distribution of food in the village. Before that, large crowds would gather outside the shops, but with the rationing system everyone was sure of getting their share."

Pawlu Aquilina recalls: "When one lived in the countryside, one could usually find something to eat although staple foods like flour, pasta and sugar were very scarce. Although there were no smokers in the family, we regularly claimed our ration of cigarettes so we could exchange them for flour and sugar with those who could not do without smoking."

As the danger of an enemy invasion increased it was decided to introduce national conscription. Regulations were published in the Government Gazette of February 20, 1941.

All men aged between 18 and 41 were subject to service in the armed forces while provision was made for the conscription of men between 16 and 56 to render service, not necessarily military.

It was made clear that conscripted men would not be called upon to serve outside Malta.

C.H. Sansom was appointed Director of Compulsory Service. Malta was divided into 10 sections with a conscription centre for each. The first group was called for March 3, 1941.

Gejtu Grech recalls: “A few days after my 18th birthday the local police sergeant called at our house and told my mother I was to consider myself under arrest. He explained to my terrified mother that though I had been repeatedly instructed by post to report at the drafting office, I had failed to turn up and in wartime such behaviour was serious. My mother immediately confessed that as she did not like the idea that I would be called up for military service she used to tear up the draft papers without telling me.

“Luckily the sergeant was a regular customer at the barber shop where I worked. He knew me well and was prepared to bend the regulations somewhat for my sake. He told me he would take no further action provided I reported at the office on the morrow.

“Early next morning I found several other young men queuing up outside. After going through the formalities and the medical test we were told to board an army truck which was to take us to Gozo...”

At the same time Malta's garrison was reinforced. On February 21, 1941, the 1st Battalion of the Cheshire Regiment arrived from Egypt. Their task was to protect the Grand Harbour and Dockyard, and also to repair RAF airfields after air raids. Two days later the 1st Battalion of the Hampshire Regiment arrived on the island, and detachments were stationed in Gudja, Żurrieq, Safi airstrip and Mqabba.

Operation Compass was the first major Allied military operation of the Western Desert campaign fought between December 1940 and February 1941. British and Commonwealth forces under General Wavell advanced from Egypt to central Libya, capturing 115,000 Italian prisoners, and destroying thousands of tanks, artillery pieces, and aeroplanes, while suffering very few casualties.

Wavell was ordered to assign a significant portion of his corps to support Greece. Hitler responded to the Italian disaster in North Africa by deploying the newly formed Deutsches Afrika Korps under General Erwin Rommel.

Rommel's first offensive started on March 24, 1941. He quickly defeated the Allied forces at El Agheila and then launched an offensive that, by April 15, pushed the British forces back to the border at Sollum, recapturing all Libya except Tobruk. Several attempts to seize Tobruk failed and the front line stabilised at the border.

Luftwaffe bombers dropped various bombs types on Malta, including aerial mines, contact mines and magnetic mines. The latter resulted in the sinking of several ships, as on April 8, 1941 when the m.v. Moor, which was employed as a boom defence vessel, hit a mine and exploded at 5.15 p.m.

The ship broke up and sank instantly. Of the 29 men on board only one survived, diver Toni Mercieca, who was picked up by a boat from the gate-vessel Westgate and conveyed to Bighi Naval Hospital.

After Italian attempts to subdue Greece failed, Hitler decided to intervene in the Balkans. On April 6, 1941, Axis forces and their Hungarian and Bulgarian allies invaded Yugoslavia from all sides and the Luftwaffe bombed Belgrade.

The Axis victory was swift. Yugoslavia surrendered in only 11 days on April 17, 1941, and was subsequently divided among Germany, Hungary, Italy and Bulgaria.

German armies then invaded Greece, and some 50,000 British and Commonwealth forces (who were helping the Greeks) had to be evacuated. The evacuation was completed on April 30, but was heavily contested by the Luftwaffe. The Germans captured around 8,000 Commonwealth soldiers.

The British Admiralty decided to base several naval units in Malta to attack Axis convoys to Libya. Four destroyers of the 14th Flotilla – HMS Jervis, HMS Janus, HMS Nubian and HMS Mohawk, known as Force K –

were sent to Malta under the command of Captain Mack, arriving on April 11, 1941.

The first success of Force K was the sinking of the Tarigo convoy off Kerkennah Islands on April 16. But the British lost HMS Mohawk.

When, on April 28, Force K was returning from a night excursion they found the 5th Destroyer Flotilla, made up of HMS Kelly, HMS Kashmir, HMS Kelvin, HMS Jersey and HMS Jackal, commanded by Captain Lord Louis Mountbatten, in Grand Harbour.

Malta was to experience a respite in attacks in mid-May 1941, when the Luftwaffe started transferring its units from Sicily; eventually, most the units of Fliegerkorps X were moved either to Greek airfields or Crete. Other units were transferred to Eastern Europe for the invasion of the Soviet Union which began on June 22.

The Regia Aeronautica quickly recovered the Sicilian airfields used by the Luftwaffe, and on May 22 Italian warplanes bombed Luqa. Meanwhile, in North Africa too, the situation was not going well for the Allies. In May 15, the British and Commonwealth forces launched Operation Brevity as a rapid blow against the weakened Axis front, but it failed to reach its aims.

The German High Command decided to invade Crete, rather than Malta, in order to secure the Balkans against British attacks on the Ploesti oilfields in Romania and also as a forward base for the invasion of Cyprus, with a final descent on the Suez Canal.

The German invasion of Crete started on May 20, 1941, with heaving strafing and bombing by waves of Luftwaffe dive-bombers and low-flying fighters. Although the Commonwealth forces defended their positions bravely causing heavy casualties on the German paratroops, the cause was hopeless and on May 27 the evacuation of the troops began. Over four nights' 16,000 troops were evacuated to Egypt by the Royal Navy. During the evacuation Luftwaffe dive-bombers sank a number of Royal Navy ships, including

HMS Kelly, where 128 survivors, including Captain Lord Louis Mountbatten, were rescued.

More than 9,000 Anzacs and thousands of Greeks were left behind. By June 1, 1941, Crete was under German control.

Meanwhile, the naval war continued and in late May a Malta-based submarine, HMS Upholder, under the command of Lieutenant Commander David Wanklyn, scored another success, after it sighted an Italian convoy consisting of the liners Conte Rosso and Victoria and the transports Marco Polo and Esperia packed with Italian troops, sailing past Syracuse.

Upholder aimed at Conte Rosso and sank the ship. In all 1,212 men perished and 1,520 were rescued.

## Malta at War Ii

### The Battle for the Mediterranean

In September and October 1941, Malta, which had by then become a prime target for Italian and German bombers, continued to be reinforced by air and sea:

fighter aircraft for the defence of the island and also another convoy to strengthen the garrison. Although air raid alarms had decreased in September, they became more frequent in the following month. At the same time, Axis convoys to North Africa were still being intercepted by air and sea from Malta.

Early in September, fighter aircraft were delivered to Malta. HMS Ark Royal sailed from Gibraltar on September 9, where during Operation Status I it flew 14 Hurricanes to Malta, and later proceeded to Egypt. Twelve Hurricanes remained aboard the aircraft-carrier. The only two Bristol Blenheims that left Gibraltar guided the 14 Hurricanes to Malta.

Then on September 13, during Operation Status II, HMS Ark Royal and HMS Furious flew off a further 46 Hurricanes to Malta. During this delivery one Hurricane crashed while taking off from Furious; it caught fire and was catapulted into the sea, but the rest reached the island safely. After their arrival, 23 of them flew on to Egypt.

In mid-September the submarines of the 10th Flotilla operating from Malta registered one of their biggest successes against the Axis convoys sent to reinforce the German Afrika Korps, led by General Erwin Rommel, in Libya. On September 17, a large Italian convoy was reported to have left Taranto; it comprised the troopships Oceania, Neptunia and Vulcania. The Royal Navy submarines Unbeaten, Upholder, Upright and Ursula were ordered to sail.

In the early morning of September 18, Upholder (Lt Cdr David Wanklyn) spotted the convoy and fired four torpedoes. Two hit the19,475-ton Neptunia and one hit the 19,507-ton Oceania. The submarine dived but later resurfaced firing two torpedoes against the stricken Neptunia, which sank in eight minutes. Two of the troopships were sunk, while Vulcania, although damaged, succeeded in reaching Tripoli. 400 out of a total of 6,900 troops perished.

Seven days later, Count Galeazzo Ciano, the Italian Foreign Minister and Benito Mussolini’s son-in-law, recorded in his diary the heavy losses sustained by Italy in terms of merchant shipping in the Mediterranean, probably referring to this episode: "Actually, the Mediterranean situation is dark, and will become even more so because of the continued loss of merchant ships. Commander Bigliardi, who is in the know and is a reliable person, says that in responsible naval circles they are seriously beginning to wonder whether we shouldn't decide to give up Libya, rather than wait until we are forced to do so by the complete lack of freighters..."

On October 1, he continued: "A conference with Admiral Ferreri. He is concerned about the fate of Libya, especially if the sinking of our merchant ships continues to be as heavy as in September. While in the past the percentage of ships lost had reached a maximum of five per cent, in September it jumped to 18 per cent..."

British Prime Minister Winston Churchill, in his six-volume memoir 'The Second World War', also mentioned the heavy losses suffered by the Axis during this period. He clearly shows the importance of Malta for the Allied cause: "...during the three months ending in September, 43 Axis ships, of 150,000 tons, besides 64 smaller craft, were sunk on the African route by British aircraft, submarines and destroyers, acting from Malta. In October, over 60 per cent of Rommel's supplies were sunk in passage..."

Churchill also said that during this time, the German admiral serving with the Italian High Command reported that "now, as ever, the British fleet dominates the Mediterranean. The Italian fleet had been unable to prevent operations by the enemy's naval forces, but, in co-operation with the Italian air force, it did prevent the Mediterranean route being used for regular British convoy traffic...

"The most dangerous British weapon is the submarine, especially those operating from Malta. In the period covered there were 36 submarine attacks; of these, 19 were successful... Owing to the weakness of the Italian air force in Sicily, the threat from Malta to the German-Italian sea route to North Africa has increased in the last few weeks..."

Due to these heavy losses, Hitler decided to send U-boats to the Mediterranean from the Atlantic. Two submarine bases were set up at La Spezia, Italy, and at Salamis in Greece for submarines in the eastern Mediterranean. The first U-boat to arrive in the Mediterranean was U-371 on September 21, followed by U-97 and U-559 on September 26, and U-331 on September 29. In October two others arrived: U-75 on October 3 and U-79 two days later.

Meanwhile, Malta received more reinforcements when the British Admiralty decided to send the convoy Operation Halberd, which consisted of nine merchant ships: HMS Breconshire, Ajax, Clan MacDonald, Clan Ferguson, Imperial Star, City of Lincoln, City of Calcutta, Dunedin Star and Rowallan Castle. The convoy sailed on September 24, 1941, from Gibraltar, with a close escort under the command of Rear Admiral Harold

Martin Burrough. It was also accompanied by Force H, under the command of Admiral Sir James Somerville. This consisted of the aircraft-carrier Ark Royal, the battleships Nelson, Rodney and Prince of Wales, five cruisers and 18 destroyers.

The Italian fleet attempted to intercept the convoy on September 26, north of Cape Ferrol, but it had already passed. When the convoy was approaching Sardinia, Italian torpedo bombers succeeded in hitting the bows of HMS Nelson which was seriously damaged on September 27. In the evening, Somerville's Force H turned back and sailed for Gibraltar and Burrough in HMS Kenya was left to escort the convoy through the Skerki Bank.

During the night, the Imperial Star was hit by Italian torpedo bombers from Pantelleria, but after an attempt to tow the merchant ship, it was sunk by HMS Oribi. The convoy reached Malta on September 28, 1941, delivering 60,000 tons of supplies. The ships between them carried 2,600 service personnel.

During the late summer and early autumn of 1941 the Regia Aeronautica stepped up its attacks on Malta following the heavy losses sustained by Italian merchant ships.

*The Axis, especially the Germans, knew this could seriously hamper their chances of winning the war in North Africa*.From September 1941, there were 31 air raid alerts over Malta, and they nearly doubled to 57 in the following month.

According to Royal Artillery statistics, during September 1941, 78 tons of bombs were dropped on Malta, mostly during nocturnal air raids. However, in October this went up to 96 tons. It is interesting to note that during this time the Italian air force employed a new fighter aircraft, the Macchi MC202 Folgore, which appeared over Malta for the first time on October 1, 1941.

To strengthen the naval forces operating from Malta against Axis convoys, the British Admiralty, at

Churchill's insistence, decided to send a small force to Malta consisting of cruisers and destroyers. This squadron, known as Force K, arrived in Malta from Gibraltar on October 21, 1941. It consisted of the cruisers Aurora and Penelope and the destroyers Lance and Lively.

The presence of Force K immediately caused problems to the Italians and, in fact, on October 22, all sea traffic across the central Mediterranean was temporarily suspended until adequate cruiser protection for their convoys could be organised.

# Malta at War III

## The Destruction Never Seemed to End

April 1942 was called l-April tat-Tnejn u Erbgħin by the Maltese because the death and destruction which occurred during this month remained in their mind for many years. The heavy attacks carried out by the German air force, the Luftwaffe, during this month were part of the assault, which became known as the

April Blitz 1942, Field Marshal Albert Kesselring's plan to neutralise Malta's ability to attack Axis convoys on their way to North Africa. Charles Grech recounts: "The first day of April 1942, happened to be Wednesday of Holy Week, when special functions are held in church, marking the start of the religious ceremonies...

"When I arrived at the junction of St Mary Street with St Trophimus Street (Sliema), where there is a niche dedicated to St Mary, Fort Manoel's guns engaged the enemy. I looked skywards to see whether anything was visible. I saw a Ju-88 approaching from the direction of Valletta, at a height of about 3,000 feet. I wanted to run for cover but I had no time so I remained where I was, clinging to the wall. I did not dare move from where I was, lest I would be machine-gunned. I saw the aircraft releasing two bombs above the submarine base at Manoel Island..."

The Maltese gunners manning the coastal and anti-aircraft guns drew widespread admiration for their dogged determination to defend their homeland.

Attacks on the island grew in intensity and on Easter Sunday (April 7), the Luftwaffe carried out 10 air raids.

One of these caused the destruction of one of Malta's architectural jewels. During the fifth air raid alert of the day, which lasted from 5.55 to 7.18 p.m., an aerial bomb hit the Royal Opera House in Valletta, demolishing it partially; debris blocked the railway tunnel shelter close by. Memè Cortis remembers that day:

"But eventually the noise subsided and the All Clear rang out. As they clambered up the steps, their first sight was of the Royal Opera House – or rather, what remained of it. This magnificent theatre, considered by many to be the finest building in Valletta, now lay in ruins. 'It was just a heap of rubble, not one wall was standing – just a few arches left. I couldn't believe it. The Royal Opera House was like Covent Garden to us.' Memè had even performed there once in a special school play..."

Initial incursions on April 9 were small, and only after midday did a large formation of enemy raiders, around 100, approach the coast, targeting the airfields. However, just before 1 p.m. around 75 aircraft made for Luqa airfield. Nine of the Stukas detached from the formation and bombed Luqa.

A large part of the parish church of St Andrew collapsed. The centre of the village was devastated, resulting in heavy casualties. Agnes Azzopardi remembers perfectly this tragic day:

"Men suddenly seemed to spring up from nowhere and rushed to the scene of the tragedy to render assistance. In the meantime bombs began to rain down again and those of us who stayed behind in the shelter feared that the people who went to help, my father among them, would be killed too. None of the men seemed to care about the great risks they were taking as they struggled to save possible survivors. In fact, there were a few survivors but 32 people died on that unforgettably tragic day."

The shelter referred to was in Pope Innocent III Street, where 23 out of 32 persons inside actually died, many of them children from the same families. Other shelters were buried under the rubble and those inside had to grope in the darkness to get out when the blast blew out the oil lamps and the candles.

After this devastation and during the same day, around 80 aircraft resumed the attacks on Ta' Qali airfield. A Junkers and a Messerschmitt were to create the legend of the miracle of the Mosta Rotunda, when at 4.40 p.m. a bomb penetrated the dome and bounced on the floor below without exploding and sparing the 300-odd worshippers there.

Other smaller calibre bombs fell at the front and at the side of the church without exploding. Anthony Camilleri wrote a book about this episode:

"Fr Salvo Sammut recalled that there were some 300 parishioners inside the temple, scattered about the floor, and the majority had moved to the side walls as the attack increased in intensity. At one stage a woman picked up her chair and ran with it into the sacristy and others followed her. As Fr Sammut himself left the confessional, several people went up to him and asked for absolution.

“At that moment a bomb pierced the roof with a loud crash, grazed the corner of the lunette with the painting of Christ and the Apostles, chipping part of the stonework, hit the ground with a bang and rolled towards the pulpit, coming to rest underneath the twelfth Station of the Cross. Several boulders rained down to reveal a large hole in the ceiling...”

Meanwhile, after Kesselring visited Cyrenaica on April 7 and 8, 1942, he reported to Hitler and Mussolini. He reported as follows to Il Duce about the success so far obtained in the offensive against Malta:

“The planned air attack on Malta between 1 and 9 has, in the opinion of the C-in-C of the Southern Area, eliminated Malta as a naval base. The shipyards and dock installations have been so badly damaged that there can be no question of using Malta as a base for a long time; the last surface forces have left Malta, and the British submarine base had been transferred to Alexandria.

"The airfields and their equipment suffered heavy damage.... C-in-C, Southern Area, intends to continue, if weather conditions permit, until April 20, and then, by continuous harassing raids, to prevent the enemy from repairing the damage..."

Kesselring's observations give an idea of Malta's situation in April 1942. For almost two years Malta had been on the frontline and was being bombarding continuously. The courage and determination of the Maltese population won widespread admiration in Britain.

It was in acknowledgment of this that in April 1942 Lieutenant-General Sir William Dobbie, the Governor of Malta, received the following message, dated April 15, 1942, from King George VI:

“To honour her brave people I award the George Cross to the Island Fortress of Malta to bear witness to a heroism and devotion that will long be famous in history.”

Governor Dobbie replied to the King with this message: “By God’s help Malta will not weaken but will endure until victory is won.” In the evening, the Governor spoke to the people over Rediffusion. Pointing out that this was the first time that an honour of this kind been bestowed by a British Sovereign on a community, Dobbie continued:

“The safety and well-being of this fortress rests, under God, on four supports. These are the three Services and the civil population. Each of them is essential to the well-being of the others, and each one depends on the other three and cannot do without them.”

The George Cross award to Malta came when in 1942 Allied fortunes were at a low ebb. The 'impregnable fortress' of Singapore had fallen to the Japanese on February 15, 1942. Other British possessions in the area had already fallen to them. The Americans were besieged at Bataan (they surrendered on April 10), and later, Corregidor (finally surrendering on May 8), and the Germans were besieging the Soviet naval base of Sevastopol, Crimea (which surrendered on July 4).

With these important Allied stands against all odds and also keeping in mind the limited military resources and food rations in Malta, the George Cross came as a morale booster both to the garrison and the civilian population of the island, collectively for the first and only time in history.

Although the two initial batches of Spitfires sent to Malta in March 1942 brought some respite, they could not operate for a long time. It was for this reason that, on April 1, 1942, Winston Churchill cabled US President

Franklin D. Roosevelt, appealing to him to permit a US carrier to be used to deliver Spitfires to Malta.

The USS Wasp was sent and the two RAF squadrons selected to go aboard the aircraft carrier were both from the Auxiliary Air Force. These were the No. 601 'County of London' and No. 603 'City of Edinburgh'. Both squadrons included pilots from Britain, the Commonwealth and North America. The aircraft were Spitfire Mk VCs.

The delivery of new Spitfires to Malta was code-named Operation 'Calendar'. The delivery took place on April 20, 1942, with the exception of one whose pilot defected and crash landed in Algeria.

The first scrambles of the day came early on April 28, two Spitfires of No. 126 Squadron and one of No. 601 Squadron going off at 7.40 a.m. They were followed 10 minutes later by four Hurricanes, to counter an estimated 43 Ju-88s, 20 Ju-87s and a large fighter escort.

Three German bombers were seen to detach themselves from the last wave, dive low over Floriana and release their bombs. One struck the dome of St Publius church, penetrated into the crypt and exploded, killing about a dozen people taking shelter, including Fr Pawlu Portelli; two other bombs also hit the church, which was severely damaged. An oral testimony cited by James Holland is that of John Agius:

"The destruction never seemed to end. One by one the famous buildings he had known all his life – buildings that represented Malta and the Maltese – were hit. He had been at work early on the 28th and after the first raid heard that the famous church of St Publius in Floriana had been hit. Standing in front of a large square, it was a sight familiar to anyone entering or leaving Valletta. John rushed up to the top of Kingsgate to see the damage for himself.

"St Publius church had a clock in each tower – one of which was never repaired. To this day it is kept at 7.50 in the morning, the time the great church was struck."

By April 29, Malta had become too precarious a base even for her successful submarine unit, 10th Submarine Flotilla, which was ordered to withdraw to Alexandria.

During April 1942 some 9,500 sorties were flown against the island and some 282 air raid alerts were sounded. Estimates of tonnes of bombs dropped ranged from 6,117 (according to the Royal Artillery) to 6,728. These bombs damaged or destroyed 11,450 buildings. A relatively low number of 297 civilians were killed and 330 seriously injured, and 208 servicemen were killed through enemy action. During the month, Malta was under alert for a total of 12 days, 10 hours and 20 minutes.

By the end of the month the Germans hardly knew where to drop their bombs. Malta's naval and air bases were put completely out of action. Ships lost in Grand Harbour during April 1942 included HMS P36 and HMS Pandora (N42) and the minesweeping drifter HMS Sunset, the minesweeper HMS Abingdon and the Royal

Hellenic Navy submarine Glaucos; the destroyers HMS Lance and Kingston; the anti-submarine trawler HMS Jade and minesweeping tug Andromeda.

On the airfields, at least 22 Spitfires and 19 Hurricanes were destroyed. The five fighter squadrons defending Malta had just seven operational Spitfires by the end of April, as well as a few Hurricanes. In April the gunners claimed 102 victories, 12 probables, and 69 damaged, against claims by the fighters for 53 shot down, 29 probables and 118 damaged.

Meanwhile, the Axis preoccupation about Malta's interference in their strategy in the central Mediterranean and North Africa and the determination to eliminate it was also confirmed on April 21, when a photo-reconnaissance Spitfire revealed a large rectangular area near Gerbini airfield in Sicily.

Two more such areas were discovered in the vicinity, parallel to the main runway, each within reach of a railway station. These areas were suspected to be glider airfields, to be used for the planned invasion of Malta.

At the same time, according to Churchill's memoirs, in early 1942 Grand Admiral Erich Raede insisted with Hitler that Malta was the key for the conquest of the Middle East: "The favourable situation in the Mediterranean, so pronounced at the present time, will probably never occur again. All reports confirm that the enemy is making tremendous efforts to pour all available reenforcements into Egypt... It is therefore imperative to take Malta as soon as possible and to launch an offensive against the Suez Canal not later than 1942."

Mussolini, who was more concerned about Malta's position and Italian losses sustained in attacks on the island, decided that all preparations for the capture of Malta should be hastened. He asked for German help, and proposed the assault for the end of May 1942.

The operation was called Operazione C3/Operation Herkules. Ugo Cavallero, the Chief of the Italian Supreme Command, offered the Italian Folgore Parachute Division of two regiments, a battalion of engineers, and five batteries. Hitler gave orders for Germans to co-operate with two parachute battalions, an engineer battalion, transport aircraft for one battalion, and by the German navy, an unspecified number of barges. However, the operation was postponed to July 1942.

The Italian Foreign Minister (and Mussolini's son-in-law) Count Galeazzo Ciano, wrote in his diary on April 28, 1942: "We leave for Salzburg. This is a meeting that was desired by the Germans, and for which, as usual, they have given us no indication of an agenda. During the journey, Cavallero talks to me about the Malta operation. He realises it is a tough nut. The preparations under way are being made with maximum attention and care, and with the conviction that the attack is essential. This is to give the maximum incentive to those concerned. But whether the operation will take place, or when, are other matters and Cavallero makes no commitments. As in his nature, he digs himself in behind a great quantity of ifs and buts..."

When the topic of the Mediterranean came up, nearly everyone agreed that Malta needed to be taken, even Rommel, who was busy planning his own offensive. Field Marshal Wilhelm Keitel also expressed difficulty providing both a division of parachutists, and the 40,000 tons of fuel oil requested for the Italian Navy. Under these circumstances, he agreed that the invasion of Malta should be postponed until after Rommel's offensive in Libya to take Tobruk. Cavallero agreed, stating that the Malta operation as a result could not be held in May, but must take place early in July.

The matter was settled with Hitler stating that the attack in Libya was to be carried out at the end of May and the attack on Malta in mid-July. Once Tobruk was taken, the bulk of the Axis air forces would be transferred back to Sicily while the Afrika Korps would dig in near Sollum on the Egyptian frontier. The leaders expected both objectives to be taken by June.

According to Hitler, however, the land war was to be decided in the East against the Soviets as only victory there would compel the British to seek terms. North Africa and Malta would contribute, but would not be the decisive blow he needed.

However, as we will see in the next features, General Erwin Rommel not only took Tobruk, but was also allowed by Mussolini and Hitler to presume his offensive against a weakened British Eighth Army, to take Suez and the Middle East oilfields.

Thus, the planned invasion of Malta was shelved and then definitely cancelled, allowing the island to take the offensive again against Axis shipping in the Central Mediterranean and determine the final outcome of the war in North Africa.

# Malta at War Iv

## Axis Plan Invasion of Malta

When Malta started to be affected by the Second World War, the Marfa-Gozo ferry service was gradually reduced from six crossings a week in 1940 to four, and eventually to two in 1941. In 1942, the service was curtailed to two morning crossings a week. On May 6, 1942, one of the ferryboats, the *Royal Lady*, was bombed in Mġarr Harbour and broke in two. Only the *Franco* and other small boats continued to operate between the two islands.

In early May 1942 it was decided to send more Spitfires to Malta. Sixty-seven Spitfires were loaded on USS *Wasp* and HMS *Eagle*. However, only 62, of which 45 were from USS *Wasp*, were delivered safely. The launching of these Spitfires, code-named Operation Bowery, coincided with the arrival of HMS *Welshman* from Gibraltar.

This mine-layer cruiser was disguised as a French cruiser, and managed to enter Grand Harbour carrying vital supplies, which apart from essential foodstuffs included fuel, ammunition and aero-engines as well as 100 RAF technicians to service the newly-arrived Spitfires. Both the warship and the Spitfires reached Malta on May 10.

The *Luftwaffe* mounted a series of raids to sink the ship in harbour. The German fighters, however, were greeted with three surprises – a highly concentrated anti-aircraft barrage, a large number of Spitfires and, for the first time, a smokescreen over Grand Harbour. There were dogfights all over the sky and Malta's defences destroyed or damaged 63 enemy aircraft.

*The cargo of HMS Welshman was completely unloaded by noon. This day became known as the Glorious Tenth of May.*

In his memoirs, British Prime Minister Winston Churchill acknowledged the turning point in the Battle of Malta: "The bombing attacks (on Malta) which had reached their peak in April (1942), now began to slacken, largely as a result of great air battles on May 9 and 10, when 60 Spitfires which had just arrived went into action with destructive effect. Daylight raiding was brought to an end."

There were 246 air raid alerts on Malta in May; during June they decreased to 169, but during July they increased again to 184. According the Royal Artillery statistics, Axis raiders dropped 628 tons of bombs on Malta, while the figure for June went down to 270 tons. However, in July, *Luftwaffe* and *Regia Aeronautica* bombers dropped 667 tons of bombs on the island.

Before Benito Mussolini's declaration of war on the Allies on June 10, 1940, a number of Maltese were studying or working in Italy. One of them was Carmelo Borg Pisani, who was born in Senglea, and who had nurtured pro-Italian sentiments since childhood. In October 1936, he was awarded a scholarship by the Italian government to study Art at the *Regia Accademia di Belle Arti* in Rome. In May 1940, he wrote to Mussolini informing him of his decision to stay in Italy to see Malta's annexation with Italy materialise.

During the night of May 17-18, 1942, Borg Pisani, using the undercover name of Caio Borghi, was brought to Malta aboard an Italian torpedo assault craft to spy for the Italians. He was landed in a dinghy and headed towards a cave at Ras id-Dawwara, between Dingli and Mtaħleb. However, within two days the sea had washed away all the items he was carrying. Realising his helplessness, he waved and shouted for help and a motor-launch was sent to pick him up.

When he arrived at Mtarfa Military Hospital he was identified by a young doctor and arrested. Borg Pisani was taken to a house at St Julian's and later transferred to a residence in Sliema, which housed Allied secret service agents, including Italians, Germans and Yugoslavs.

In conjunction with this spying mission, as the Axis powers were preparing to invade Malta, on April 29-

30, Adolf Hitler and Mussolini met in Salzburg, Austria, to discuss their Mediterranean strategy. It was decided to take first Tobruk in Libya and then Malta. The island's invasion, codenamed Operation Herkules by the Germans and C3 by the Italians, would take place only after the British forces in North Africa had been beaten.

In the early months of 1942 the German air force's *Fliegerkorps II* mounted heavy attacks on Malta to neutralise its defences and demoralise the population. By May 10, the German commander in the Mediterranean, Albert Kesselring, regarded the task as accomplished and*Fliegerkorps II* started moving from Sicily to North Africa.

On May 26, Erwin Rommel duly attacked, and by June 21 Tobruk was in Axis hands. According to his directive, Rommel should have halted, and the forces should have been reorganised for the invasion of Malta. Instead, Hitler permitted Rommel to continue his advance to the Suez Canal.

This decision is generally considered as the end of Operation Herkules. However, Hitler was reluctant to lose more paratroops, as had happened during the airborne invasion of Crete in May 1941, and alternative plans for the invasion of Malta were drawn up.

The invasion force, under the command of General Student, was to consist of the Seventh *Fallschirmjäger* (paratroops) Division and the 66th Special Purpose Panzer Company, chosen to deal with the strong anti-tank defences on the island. These tanks were to be landed by barges in Marsaxlokk Bay.

There would be also a *Gebirgsjäger* (mountain) Division. These troops were to be carried by 500 Junkers and 12 Messerschmitt Me323, 300 DFS230 and 200 new Gotha Go242, 216 fighters as escort and 200 other mixed aircraft.

The Italians were to contribute the Folgore Division and La Spezia Infantry Division. The *Regia Aeronautica* would supply some 222 fighters plus 470 mixed bombers, while the *Regia Marina* would contribute five battleships, four heavy cruisers, 21 destroyers and 14 submarines. In total, some 30,000 men were to be made available for the airborne assault, plus a further 70,000 to follow by sea.

To help the Axis invading troops a *Centro Militare G* was established, consisting of a number of Maltese (living in Italy) and Italians, led by Captain Lamberto Negri. They were to act as guides and interpreters to the Axis invading forces during the invasion.

The landings were planned to be made on the south-west coast of Malta on July 18, 1942, in the area between Wied iż-Żurrieq and Għar Lapsi. The Qrendi airfield and any anti-aircraft positions in the area would be captured and held. However the unexpected capture of Tobruk and Hitler's permission to Rommel to continue advancing into Egypt led to the shelving of the plan to invade Malta.

In May 1942, the Admiralty decided to send two simultaneous convoys to Malta from both ends of the Mediterranean. The convoy from the west, known as Operation Harpoon, left Scotland on June 4,1942. It consisted of the freighters *Burdwan*, *Chant* (American), *Orari*,*Tanimbar* (Dutch) and *Troilus*, joined during the night of June 11-12 by the American tanker *Kentucky*.

On June 14 the convoy was attacked by the *Luftwaffe* and the *Regia Aeronautica* and*Tanimbar* was sunk. Early next morning, the convoy was attacked by an Italian cruiser squadron. As the surviving ships were approaching Grand Harbour during midnight of June 15-16, *Orari*, HMS *Matchless*, HMS *Badsworth*, ORP *Kujawiak* (a Polish destroyer) and HMS*Hebe* hit mines, but only the Polish destroyer sank.

The *Luftwaffe* did not attack the two freighters *Orari* and *Troilus* in harbour, and in five days a total of 13,532 tons of cargo were unloaded.

The second convoy, known as Operation Vigorous, was less fortunate. The freighters *Aagtekirk, Buthan, City of Calcutta* and *Rembrandt* departed from Port Said on June 11; the freighters *Ajax, City of Edinburgh,City of Lincoln, City of Pretoria* and *Elizabeth Bakke* (Norwegian) left Haifa the following day, while the freighter *Potaro* and the tanker *Bulkoil* left Alexandria on the 13th.

The three branches joined up into one convoy during the afternoon of June 13, north of Tobruk. After suffering several losses in *Luftwaffe* attacks, and also with the intervention of the Italian navy, the remaining ships turned back to Alexandria. During their return voyage the British also lost the cruiser HMS *Hermione,* which was sunk by the German submarine U-205.

The failure to sufficiently reinforce Malta deeply worried Churchill. In his words, during June 1942, "in spite of our greatest efforts only two supply ships out of 17 got through, and the crises in the island continued".

With the failure to reinforce Malta sufficiently, Churchill was preoccupied about the island's ability to continue to resist Axis attacks. However, as will be seen next week, a large convoy was to be sent to Malta in mid-August 1942, to resupply the island at all costs

# Malta at War V

## The Convoy that Saved Malta from Surrender

In 2012 Malta is celebrating the 70th anniversary of the award of the George Cross on April 15, 1942, and the arrival of the convoy codenamed Operation Pedestal, commonly known as the Santa Marija Convoy, on August 15 of that year. These are probably the two most important dates highlighting Malta's role during World War II, which determined the outcome of the North African campaign and the war in the Mediterranean, and the surrender of Italy nearly a year later, on September 8, 1943.

As Malta edged inevitably towards starvation and surrender in the summer of 1942, a major naval undertaking was being put in train to enable Malta to survive. The suspension of Arctic convoys until the shortening days of autumn released a number of warships from the British Home Fleet for service in support of Operation Pedestal.

On June 18, 1942, British Prime Minister Winston Churchill was in Washington, where the chiefs-of-staff cabled him, urging him to request the loan of the tanker SS Ohio, on the same basis as SS Kentucky. Also requested from the American administration were two other merchant ships, Santa Elisa and Almeria Lykes. The remaining merchant ships were British and all of them were armed with anti-aircraft guns. A large escorting force was assembled to protect the convoy, comprising two main groups of ships, Forces Z and X.

The overall operational commander was Vice-Admiral E.N. Syfret. The convoy was codenamed WS.5.21.S. Just prior to sailing, Rear-Admiral Burrough met with the Convoy Commodore A.G. Venables, and the masters of the individual merchant ships on board his flagship.

The convoy entered the Mediterranean on the night of August 10, 1942. Its codename became Operation Pedestal. Protecting the vessels, the Royal Navy had the three aircraft carriers HMS Eagle, HMS Victorious and HMS Indomitable, the battleships HMS Nelson and HMS Rodney, besides seven cruisers, 32 destroyers, eight submarines and other units.

The following is a chronology of events following the departure of the convoy from Gibraltar:

Wednesday, August 11
1.15 p.m.: The German submarine U-73 fires four torpedoes into HMS Eagle, sinking it in eight minutes. Some 927 survivors out of 1,160 officers and men were picked up from the sea by the tug HMS Jaunty and two destroyers, HMS Lookout and HMS Laforey.

2.50 p.m.: HMS Furious successfully flies off 38 much-needed Spitfires to Malta (Operation Bellows).

Thursday, August 12
4.16 p.m.: The Italian submarine Axum fires four torpedoes and hits three ships, two of which are HMS Nigeria and the anti-aircraft cruiser HMS Cairo, severely damaging the latter. Cairo had to be sunk by gunfire from HMS Derwent north of Bizerte.

8.50 p.m.: MV Empire Hope suffers 18 near misses before a bomb bursts a stove in its side, stopping the engines. In seconds, ammunition fuel and aviation spirit explode, setting the stern of the vessel ablaze. The crew abandon ship and are picked up by HMS Penn, the latter firing a torpedo into the doomed merchant ship to sink.

9.20 p.m.: Two Junkers Ju88s attack Deucalion. One bomb strikes the ship, a tremendous fire breaks out and the aviation spirit and kerosene explode. Captain Brown orders abandon ship and HMS Bramham approaches the merchantman to pick up survivors.

Friday, August 13

12.40 a.m.: The first torpedo attack by Italian MAS-boats and German Schnellboote in the narrows between Pantelleria and the Tunisian coast. MS 22 and MS 16 speed towards the passing cruiser HMS Manchester, loose their torpedoes and withdraw into the darkness. Seconds later Manchester is hit in the starboard side.

Later, many of the survivors reach Tunisia and are taken prisoner by the Vichy French, who intern them in Bon Fichu, with the survivors from MV Glenorchy and MV Clan Ferguson.

2 a.m.: MV Glenorchy is hit by torpedoes from the Italian torpedo boat MS 31. Captain Leslie, mindful of the aviation spirit stowed all over the deck, orders his men to abandon ship. Some 124 souls, including the 25 passengers, survive the attack and are ordered to take the boats. MS 31 approaches the sinking ship and picks Chief Officer Hanney and eight men as prisoners.

3 a.m.: A second wave of Italian MAS-boats and German Schnellboote attack the convoy. MAS 552 and MAS 554 torpedo the Wairangi in its port side. Captain Gordon decides to scuttle the ship. The boats are lowered and later the ship is sunk.

3.30 a.m.: Schnellboote S30 and S36 torpedo the American Almeria Lykes and the ship is hit forward in No. 1 hold, where a stow of bags of flour absorbs much of the explosion. However, Captain Henderson orders the crew to abandon ship and 105 men board three boats.

4.15 a.m.: An Italian torpedo boat, MAS 564, closes in from the starboard side of the American ship Santa Elisa and fires a torpedo at point-blank range. The detonation takes place amid aviation spirit. The master orders the crew to abandon ship and the survivors are picked up by HMS Penn.

8 a.m.: Two Junkers Ju88s make a concentrated attack against Waimarama. Four bombs explode amid spirit

and ammunition. A vast sheet of flame roars high up into the sky. The survivors are picked up by HMS Ledbury.

6.30 p.m.: Rochester Castle, Port Chalmers and Melbourne Star enter Grand Harbour. As the battle-scarred vessels slide between the arms of the breakwater, the Royal Malta Artillery band plays from the ramparts of Fort St Elmo to welcome the surviving ships.

Saturday, August 14
6 a.m.: Brisbane Star, which was hit by a torpedo two days before, has been sailing independently, heading round Cape Bon and keeping inshore. Spitfires fly over the ship and remain flying over until it enters the harbour early in the afternoon.

9.55 a.m.: HMS Tartar sinks HMS Foresight with a torpedo and heads at high speed to Gibraltar.

11 a.m.: Captain Tucket of Dorset orders the crew to abandon ship and they board the boats. During the evening the ship is hit by bombs and sinks.

11.30 a.m.: A tremendous effort is made to tow the crippled tanker Ohio into harbour. Speed is worked up to a gratifying six knots, with a steady enough course. Morale rises accordingly and to cheer everyone up, Chattanooga Choo-Choo, is played loudly from HMS Penn's PA system.

Sunday, August 15
2 a.m.: With HMS Penn and HMS Bramham edging Ohio along the shore, HMS Ledbury lends its power to shove the tanker's bow to make the turns off Delimara and Żonqor Points.

8 a.m.: On the feast of Santa Marija (the Assumption of Our Lady), the broken-backed and almost derelict hull of Ohio makes the tight turn inside the mole, rounds Ricasoli Point and heads up Grand Harbour. The crews on the ships are greeted by crowds, cheering deliriously, lining the ramparts and bastions while

bands play God Save the King, The Star-Spangled Banner and Rule Britannia. However, at the same time Maltese children start shouting "We want food, not oil!"

Tears sting red-rimmed eyes as the Ohio proceeds towards Parlatorio Wharf in French Creek.

Churchill recognised the sacrifices made to resupply Malta at all costs: "In the end five gallant merchant ships out of 14 got through with their precious cargoes. The loss of 350 officers and men and of so many of the finest ships in the merchant navy and in the fleet of the Royal Navy was grievous.

"The reward justified the price exacted. Revictualled and replenished with ammunition and vital stores, the strength of Malta revived. British submarines returned to the island, and, with the striking forces of the Royal Air Force, regained their dominating position in the Central Mediterranean."

As Operation Pedestal drew to a close, the unloading of the merchant ships, code-named Operation Ceres, also reached its final phase. The cargoes of Port Chalmers, Rochester Castle and Melbourne Star had been unloaded, and the discharge of Ohio and Brisbane Star was rapidly completed. For the authorities, the 568 Pedestal survivors remained a liability, and they were moved out of Malta as quickly as possible.

*Although 53,000 of the 85,000 tons of supplies loaded on the merchant ship finished on the bottom of the Mediterranean, the remaining 32,000 tons enabled Malta to stave off the target date for the island's surrender, which was the first week of September 1942.*

# Malta at War Vi

## Siege of Malta Lifted in November 1942

The first day of November 1942 started with a scramble at 12.05pm by four Spitfires of No. 1435 Squadron to investigate a raid which did not materialise.

In North Africa, as the British Eighth Army at last had broken through during the Second Battle of El Alamein on November 6, 16 Beaufighters of No. 272 Squadron flew to Ta' Qali from Egypt, followed by six Wellingtons of No. 104 Squadron, which flew to Luqa airfield. They arrived in Malta to lend support to the next Allied operation in North Africa, the Anglo-American invasion of French North Africa, which was held by Vichy France, allied to Germany.

On November 8, the Anglo-Americans launched a three-pronged amphibious landing, codenamed Operation Torch, to seize the key ports and aerodromes of Morocco and Algeria simultaneously, targeting Casablanca, Oran and Algiers. The only fighting took place in the port of Algiers itself. General Juin surrendered the city to the Allies two days later. By now, Hitler ordered the occupation of Vichy France and reinforced Axis forces in Africa.

Meanwhile, in Egypt an attempt was made to encircle the Axis forces at Marsa Matruh but the Allied attack was frustrated by rain and the Afrika Korps succeeded to escape by November 7. Tobruk was retaken on November 13, but Field Marshal Erwin Rommel's forces escaped the trap again, and Benghazi fell on November 20.

The Germans and Italians retired to a prepared defence line at El Agheila. Axis supplies and reinforcements were now directed into Tunisia at Rommel's expense. Since Rommel's supply lines by sea had become so perilous, more and more material had to be transported by air. The Axis could only succeed in this if the aerial convoy was protected by a heavy fighter escort.

Hitler ordered that the El Agheila line should be held at all costs. However, Rommel's view was for a fighting retreat to Tunisia and a strong defensive position at the Gabès Gap. Permission was granted for a withdrawal to Buerat, east of Sirte. An attempt to outflank El Agheila between December 14 and 16 once again failed to encircle the enemy, and Rommel's forces withdrew.

Meanwhile, in Malta, fuel supplies as well as other vital stores were again running low. No supplies in appreciable quantity had been received since Operation Pedestal (Santa Marija convoy, mid-August) and there was again the need for another convoy. However, before another operation could be mounted, alternative steps were taken to send supplies to Malta.

In October, the submarines HMS Parthian and HMS Clyde made a trip each from Gibraltar, bringing in aviation spirit, diesel and lubricating oils, torpedoes and foodstuffs. More aviation spirit and torpedoes were delivered by the two submarines in November.

That month an attempt was made to send three unescorted and disguised merchant ships. Empire Patrol sailed from Alexandria, Egypt, with a cargo of aviation spirit and benzene. She was spotted by a

German aircraft near Cyprus where she put to port due to engine trouble.

Two other merchant ships, Ardeola and Tadorna, entered the Mediterranean bound for Malta with foodstuffs. At first they formed part of Operation Torch, but as soon they detached themselves from the invasion force, both ships were stopped and boarded, the crew being interned by the Vichy French.

Although the British Admiralty suffered these setbacks, the chiefs-of-staff in London were determined to resupply Malta. HMS Manxman and HMS Welshman were again loaded with reinforcements and sent to Malta. The first reached the island on November 12 with 350 tons of foodstuffs, while Welshman arrived on November 18.

Yet another convoy was being prepared for Malta. The freighters of convoy Operation Stoneage started loading at Port Sudan. The merchant ships included Bantam (Dutch), Denbighshire, Mormacmoon and

Robin Locksley (American). The freighters passed the Suez Canal, reaching Port Said on November 16, after which they headed westwards along the Egyptian coast. The next day the Mediterranean Fleet left Alexandria to join the convoy; it consisted of the cruisers Cleopatra (flagship Rear-Admiral Power), Arethusa, Dido, Orion and nine destroyers, and they were later joined by another seven destroyers.

Early on November 18, the convoy was discovered by a German aircraft and was attacked at about 3pm. Three hours later it was again attacked by German torpedo-bombers off Derna, hitting Arethusa on the port side. The cruiser, escorted by the destroyer Petard, turned back towards Alexandria at slow speed.

At about 2pm the following day the convoy reached a position about 80 miles south-east of Malta, and Cleopatra, Dido, Orion and the six fleet destroyers turned back to Alexandria. Euryalus and the nine Hunt destroyers continued to escort the convoy to Malta.

On November 20, the convoy started entering Grand Harbour, bringing some 28,861 tons of supplies. *The supplies brought to Malta by convoy Operation Stoneage postponed Malta's capitulation date to late January 1943. This convoy effectively lifted the siege of Malta*.

By the end of the month and early December, another convoy, Operation Portcullis was prepared to reinforce Malta. On November 30 the American tanker Yorba Linda left Port Said for Benghazi escorted by four destroyers and some corvettes. The next day, convoy Operation MW14 departed from Port Said. It consisted of the freighters Alcoa Prospector and Agwimonte (both American), Glenartney and Suffolk, escorted by four destroyers.

Then a day later, the cruiser HMS Orion, accompanied by six destroyers, left Alexandria, joining the convoy in the early morning. At about 5pm of December 3, Force K, consisting of the cruisers Cleopatra, Dido and Euryalus left Grand Harbour with four destroyers and went cruising in the lower Ionian Sea as distant protection for the convoy.

At about noon the convoy met with the tanker Yorba Linda and her escorts off the hump of Cyrenaica. Then the whole convoy set out in a north-westerly direction towards Malta. On the evening of December 4, Force K returned to Malta, while by nightfall, convoy Operation MW14 started entering Grand Harbour. The last of the destroyers did not enter harbour until about 5am of December 5.

The convoy brought about 28,000 tons of supplies. Operation MW14 or Portcullis can be considered as the last of the 'Malta Convoys' which set out specifically with Malta as the only destination.

The three convoys which reached Malta during November and December 1942 suffered no damage and the rations were progressively raised until an all-round increase was possible at the beginning of January.

On November 21 it was announced that the changes in the arrangements for Victory Kitchens would take place as from January 23, 1943.

One month was given to the public to decide whether to draw their food entirely in the form of rations or partly as rations and partly through the Victory Kitchens. This announcement was widely welcomed and led to a drop in registrations until the Communal Feeding Department was closed in September 1943.

Meanwhile, aerial pressure against Malta continued to ease. During November there was a large reduction of air raid alerts from 153 in October to 30 in November, but slightly increased again to 35 in December. In fact, the last air raid alert of 1942 was recorded during the night of 17/18 December. It was a heavy raid by 40 Junkers Ju88 which bombed Luqa, Qrendi, Siġġiewi, Gudja and Safi. At about 4am of the 18th, a Handley Page Halifax of No.138 Squadron, flew low over Żejtun with engines failing and crashed between Il-Bajjada and Ta' San Girgor, east of Żejtun.

The bomber was carrying passengers from the Middle East to the United Kingdom. Seventeen Royal Air Force, Polish Air Force and British Army personnel lost their lives.

According to the Royal Artillery statistics, during October, around 624 tons of bombs were dropped on Malta, while in November only 12 tons of bombs were recorded, which increased again to 60 tons during December.

According to the same statistics, during 1942 some 12,179 tons had been dropped on Malta and Gozo, the worst month being April, which totalled some 6,117, followed by March with 2,028 and February with 1,020 tons of bombs respectively.

The end of 1942 saw an increase in terms of bombers and torpedo-bombers stationed in Malta. More Wellingtons, Albacores and Beaufighters flew in from the Middle East, while Mosquito Mk.IIs from No.23

Squadron were based in Malta, the first aircraft of its type to operate from outside Britain.

## History of the Jews in Malta

The history of the Jews in Malta can be traced back to approximately 60 AD. The first Jew known to have set foot on Malta was Paul of Tarsus, whose ship foundered there in 60 AD. Paul went on to introduce Christianity to the island population.

Greek inscriptions and menorah-decorated tombs indicate that Jews and early Christians lived on Malta during the fourth and fifth centuries AD. During the Arab rule of the island Jews often held posts as civil servants; one member of the community even reaching the highest possible rank, Vizier.

The Jewish population of Malta peaked in the Middle Ages under Norman rule. The Normans occupied the islands from 1091, with five hundred Jews living on the main island and 350 on the sister island, Gozo. The Jewish people generally prospered during this period and were not required to live in ghettos. Most owned agricultural land or worked as merchants. Abraham Abulafia, a well-known Jewish mystic, lived on Comino from 1285 to his death in the 1290s.

In 1435 the *Università* demanded the abolition of a tax which was due to be imposed on the Jews. This was well appreciated by the Jewish Community in Malta and Gozo and a Gozitan Jew named Xilorun was chosen as an ambassador of the Maltese Deputies to the court of Sicily. In 1479 Malta and Sicily came under Aragonese rule and the 1492 Edict of Expulsion forced all Jews to leave the country. Because they made up such a large portion of the island's population the Spanish Crown forced them to pay compensation for the losses caused by their expulsion.

It is not clear where the Jews of Malta went, but they may have joined the Sicilian community in Levant. It is also likely that several dozen Maltese Jews converted to Christianity to remain in the country as did many Sicilian Jews. This is further evidenced by the large number of Maltese surnames thought to be of Jewish origin.

In the medieval era when Mdina was Malta's capital, one-third of its population was Jewish. A synagogue inside Mdina was destroyed by an earthquake in 1693. Deeds and other documents written by Jewish notaries in Maltese with Hebrew script are today located in the Mdina Cathedral Museum. They are amongst the earliest known Maltese language texts, dating back to the 14th century.

In 1530 Charles V of Spain gave Malta to the Knights of Saint John. The Knights ruled the island until 1798; many Sicilian *conversos* then moved here remembering the Knights' liberal policy towards the Jews of Rhodes, but they had to continue practicing their religion in secrecy. Jews volunteered for the desperate attempt to relieve Fort St Elmo during the Great Siege. Following this, was no free Jewish population in the country during the Knights' reign. The Knights would often take passengers of merchant ships - including numerous

Jews - hostage in order to get the ransom and it would be up to Jewish Societies for the Redemption of Captives to raise it. There were therefore many Jewish slaves in Malta during this period and Malta was frequently mentioned for its large enslaved Jewish population in Jewish literature of the period. Free Jews wishing to visit the country could only enter through one port in Valletta, which is still known as the *Jews' Sallyport*.

With Napoleon Bonaparte slavery in Malta was abolished and thus, it then became possible for a free Jewish community to exist once again. Hence, Jewish settlers began to arrive shortly afterwards. The majority of the contemporary Maltese Jewish community originates in Jewish immigration from Gibraltar, England, North Africa, Portugal and Turkey during the short period of French rule from 1798 to 1800 and British rule after that. From 1805 Jews were the targets of campaigns by the Maltese directed at all foreigners. In 1846, a Tripolitania became the country's first modern *rabbi*.

During the early 20th century the island did not always have a rabbi of its own and rabbis would be flown in from Sicily to perform ceremonies. In the time before World War II many Jews fleeing Nazism came to Malta as it was the only European country not to require visas of Jews fleeing German rule. Numerous Maltese Jews fought Germany in the British Army during the war.

# The Re-Christianisation of Malta

## Siculo-Greek Monasticism, Dejr Toponyms and Rock-Cut Churches

### The Re-Christianisation Process

In 1896, A. Mayr argued convincingly for a bishopric of Malta in 1156.There is, none the less, no secure mention of a bishop until June 1168 when Johannes, Bishop of Malta, petitioned the Royal Exchequer in Palermo for the grant of approximately a quarter of an acre of arable land to set up an endowment in favour of the newly built church of the Saviour at Capizzi, near Cefalú. Johannes can be documented in Sicily until 1212, but nothing is known of his Maltese activities. The unnamed bishop of Malta mentioned on 1st December 1217, in the registers of Pope Honorius III, could have been Johannes's successor. A mention in 1244, in a *diploma* in the Archivio Capitolare of Palermo, of a Johannes Zafarana *Maltensis canonicus*, may suggest an organized diocese, but this cannot be confirmed until around 1270 when Malta had passed under Angevin rule. The ecclesiastical establishment seems to have consisted of a Latin-rite Sicilian clergy based at Mdina where there was certainly a cathedral church by 1299. The presence of Latin Christianity is also apparent at the Castrum Maris on the Grand Harbour, where a Latin-rite church of Santa Maria is documented in 1274, and in the Gozo castello where the *miles* Guillelmus de Malta, nephew of Andrea, Count of Malta, lay dying in 1299.

It seems probable that in Malta, as on the island of Pantalleria, the three-pronged programme of Christianisation and Latinisation, linguistic assimilation, and cultural acclimatization, was, in comparison with Sicily, unduly delayed. Until the forced expulsion of the Muslim community, which has recently been tentatively relocated to the period 1221 – 1225, their inhabitants were *tam christiani quam saraceni*. The available evidence suggests that Christianity was defiantly resisted by the Muslim natives, many of whom, as in Sicily, found refuge in the countryside where they could perpetuate their religion and cultural traditions with less molestation. It is unclear if the policy of religious toleration encouraged by the Norman Court at Palermo was practiced in Malta.

The isolated reference, in an official diploma of 1198 to a collective fine imposed on the Christian community for the murder of a Muslim, is open, as shown by C. Dalli, to different interpretations.The Muslim population seems to have formed a distinct class and, perhaps, as happened on Pantalleria, had some sort of local council based on Islamic customs.There is reason to believe that their status was inferior to that of the Latin Christian community, and that this state of affairs continued to be reflected long after 1225 when fear of exile to Lucera, in Apuglia, coerced an apparently substantial number into accepting baptism.

A measure of social inequality was also apparently manifest between the Latin and Greek clergy present on Malta in the 12th and 13th centuries. There is as yet no conclusive documentary evidence of the activities of a Greek monastic network, but its presence is reliably indicated by a number of eloquent non-written sources that include iconographic, architectural, hagiographic, and toponomastic evidence. Its work, and theological and liturgical idiosyncrasies must necessarily be viewed in the context of Sicily of which Malta was a geographic, political, and (to an extent) ethnic appendage. There are undeniable pitfalls in such an approach, and one should guard oneself against going too far, but the fundamental importance of a sound understanding of the situation prevailing in Sicily at a time when its relations with Malta were especially intimate, cannot be sufficiently stressed. Siculo-Greek monasticism had, in addition, a missionary dimension and founded affiliated houses on the island of Pantalleria, in the Calabria and Basilicata regions of mainland Italy, and as far away as Mount Athos in Greece. The probability of a monastery on Malta before 1300 has already been hinted at by H. Bresc. This study seeks to consolidate the arguments and discuss the corroborating evidence.

## Siculo-Greek Monasticism

Greek-monasticism in Sicily has its roots in the ascetic coenobitic tradition of the early Christian period, and benefited from contacts with the Orient, particularly the Nile Delta and Syria.This experience resulted in a fascination with escathology and anchoritic activity that is often reflected in the rock-cut hermitages, and in the architecture of some of the built churches particularly in eastern Sicily. Syrian architectural influence seems, in particular, to receive a measure of support from the 8th century *Vita* of SS. Alphio, Philadelphius, and Tecla which tells of three Syrian master masons who arrived unexpectedly to build a church founded by Tecla at Lentini, where their arrival was regarded as miraculous because of the absence in Sicily of competent architects. The predilection for cave-hermitages is similarly corroborated by the *Lives* of other Sicilian-Greek saints, such as Gregorius Decapolita, and Calogero, who followed the example of Philip of Agira and went to live in a cave. Philip of Agira, whose father was allegedly a Syrian animal merchant, was a central figure to Sicilian-Greek monasticism and the famous monastic establishment on the slopes of Mount Etna, founded on the site where according to a legend already current in the 8th century, the saint had performed his most spectacular miracles, remained a point of reference throughout the Muslim period and the Norman government that succeeded it. His cult in Malta, which may be the only one outside Sicily and the Calabria, is, in spite of its uncertain origins, of notable significance.

In the Norman period, the Sicilian-Greek monasteries that had survived the long Muslim rule were more remarkable for their asceticism and piety than as centers of learning and theological study. The cultural poverty was, to an extent, the result of a diaspora of scholars and erudite clergy who, after the Islamic conquest, had sought refuge in more secure provinces of the Empire. Enclaves of Sicilian-Greeks in exile were, in this way, formed in Constantinople and the Peloponese, and, possibly, also in Rome.

The most important exodus was, presumably, however, to South Italy, particularly the Calabria and Basilicata region.In Muslim Sicily, Christianity was tolerated, but the Christian community suffered injustices and was often discriminated against. The monasteries continued to exist but suffered harassment, and there is evidence for at least one martyrdom, that of the monk Argenzius which took place in Palermo in the Spring of 906. The hub of Greek monasticism remained Eastern Sicily, particularly the areas round Syracuse, the Val Demone and the Val di Noto where the ascetic and troglodytic traditions remained one of the essential characteristics. The intellectual revival that manifested itself at the turn of the 12th century, in the wake of the Norman conquest, was in great measure achieved by the migration of Calabrian monks who sometimes carried valuable books in their luggage. These monks grafted on to the Sicilian-Byzantine tradition new devotional and religious idiosyncrasies, one of which was the cult of the obscure Irish saint Catald that centred round the Port city of Taranto. It was through this channel that Catald came to be venerated in Malta where a partially rock-cut church was built above an early Christian cemetery in Rabat.

**The Dejr Toponyms**

In 1647 Giovanni Francesco Abela argued for an early 12th century Benedictine house on Malta on the basis of a notice in the martyrology of the Benedictine congregation of Pulsano in Calabria. It is, however, almost certain that the *Melita Insula* mentioned in the document was the nearby Dalmatian Island of Melida in the Adriatic that was owned by the monks of Pulsano who founded a monastery there in 1151. There is in fact no evidence for Latin monasticism in Malta prior to the late 14th century, and it is significant that in 1363 the Benedictines of San Nicolò l'Arena at Catania turned down a pious endowment for the setting up of a house on Malta on the principal pretext that the island had "no buildings in which the brethren could conduct the monastic life of prayer, meditation, reading, and teaching". The other reasons included the fact that the language spoken by the natives was alien to the monks and that the journey to the island was too hazardous.

Hints of eastern monastic establishments may, on the other hand, be contained in the several *Dejr*-toponyms encountered in different parts of Malta but not,apparently, on Gozo. *Dejr* (derived from the Arabic*dayr*) normally means a Christian monastic set-up,and G.B. Pellegrini records three Sicilian *Dejr*-toponyms which clearly refer to monasteries. It can, however, as G. Wettinger has pointed out, have other interpretations, foremost among them that of a sheepfold. The two meanings were, in fact, sometimes combined, as in the case of the Tunisian island of Galita where there is a late medieval reference to a convent known as the 'Convent of the Sheep'. The issue at stake is whether the Maltese *Dejr*-toponyms derive from the presence of early post-Muslim monasteries, or whether they record the presence of sheepfolds. Wettinger who published his first pioneering study in 1974, has wisely cautioned prudence, and is sceptical of religious associations, arguing that the surviving toponyms have no apparent connections with either cloistered buildings or churches. His hypothesis is justified if considered exclusively in the context of Latin Christianity. With the significant exception of Abbatija tad-Dejr, there is, in fact, no evidence of a link with

Latin monasticism, and some of the toponyms, such as Dejr il-Bniet (first recorded in 1351),or Dejr Baqar, and Dejr Handun (both first recorded in 1399) were seemingly already well established when the Western Orders started making a presence in last decades of the 14th century. If therefore the Maltese *Dejr* were as a monastic building, as was the case in Sicily, an earlier and different type of monasticism would seem indicated.

**The Abbatija tad-Dejr**

The only *Dejr*-place-name with uncontested Christian associations is Abbatija tad-Dejr at Rabat where the site centres around an early Christian cemetery that is first described in 1647 by G.F. Abela who refers to it as a "Cimiterio nominato l'Abbatia". The name which, at first sight, has the significance of being compounded of a Romance word and its Semitic equivalent, is of unknown antiquity, but the area can presumably be identified with the *clausura* 'Ta' l-Abbatija *in contrata iddeyr'*, mentioned in a deed of 1549 when it formed part of the landed property of the Benedictine nuns of St. Peter, at Mdina. The fact that the appellative 'Ta' l-Abbatija' does not feature in an earlier reference to the district, in an act of 1467,may arguably suggest that it was added to qualify property rights after they had been acquired by the nuns.

The place has notable archaeological and art historical significance and consists of an early Christian necropolis, made up of a main cemetery (Hypogeum I) with sixteen freestanding baladacchino-tombs, and of three smaller hypogea (II – III- IV), dug into the sides of a low hill that was quarried to enclose a quadrangular space. A colonnaded building with an *opus sectile* floor, fronted the complex, and Hypogeum 1 was in turn accessed through a rock-cut oratory. The dating evidence is insecure. A chi-rho monogram on one of the baldacchino-tombs excludes a date prior to the mid-4th century, but burials were taking place around the 5th, when a Latin inscription recording several deceased was painted in red ochre on a tomb in

Hypogeum IV. Architectural and artistic considerations suggest that the site had a gradual development and a long life that spilled beyond the start of the Byzantine period around 535 A.D.

In the post-Muslim period, the site was revitalized as a cult centre and as a monastic (possibly anchoritic) station by an ascetic religious community whose Sicilian-Greek roots are indicated by the stylistic idiosyncrasies of their architectural interventions, and the wall icons that they painted. Both have a close affinity with the Basilian troglodytic coenobitic establishments that flourished in Sicily, and the Apuglia, Basilicata, and Calabria, regions in the Norman and Swabian periods, between the late eleventh and the late thirteenth centuries.There is in particular, as noted by Aldo Messina, a close similarity to the Grotta dei Santi at Monterosso Almo, in the province of Ragusa where a Paleochristian hypogeum was likewise adapted to the needs of a monastic community.The monks squatted among the tombs and Hypogeum III was transformed into a monastic cell that preserves the sinopia of two haloed heads that probably belonged to an icon of two standing saints painted for the private contemplation of the resident monk. The oratory at the entrance to Hypogeum I was likewise decorated with icons that included a *St John the Evangelist* and a *St. Michael the Archangel* (known through 19th century photographs), and a probable *Christ Pantocrator* whose sinopia survives in a poor state of preservation. Greek crosses with forked finials, highlighted with red paint, were deeply incised on the walls.

A paleochristian burial-chamber at right angles to Hypogeum (I) was meanwhile mutilated and transformed into a modestly proportioned oratory (3.20m x 2.89m) that was still in use as a church, under the dedication of the Nativity of the Virgin, in 1575. It has a flat ceiling supported by a rock-pillar (that was presumably re-cut from a baldacchino-tomb), and low, partially built benches along the side walls. The back wall had an apsed recess, 1.21m deep, with a Siculo-Byzantinesque mural that telescoped into a single scene the principal Christian mysteries of the Annunciation and the Crucifixion. Stylistic and iconographic evidence exclude a date prior to the late 13th century, and there is an evident stylistic relationship to a thematically related painting in the, already mentioned, Grotta dei Santi at Monterosso Almo, in Ragusa.On the rock-pilaster were two armorial shields one of which carried the arms of the Kingdom of Sicily, and the other had a white cross on a red field that looked suspiciously similar to the standard of the Knights of St. John.Both are presumably late additions and may in fact belong to a post-1530 period.

## The Eschatological Dimension of Troglodytic Monasticism

Abbatija tad-Dejr is an important example of the widely diffused phenomenon of rock-cut churches and troglodytic monasticism that manifested itself in many places of the Mediterranean littoral during the Middle Ages. Peter Brown has perceptively categorized it as an important aspect of an early pan-Mediterranean monastic culture that bore witness to the horizontal unity of the Middle Sea because it was unaware of any distinction between East and West. The practice may have stemmed from the East where it could have had an eschatological significance because of its symbolic association with the tomb and, therefore with death that man must undergo to wake up to eternal life.

Michael Gervers sees in it an allegorical image in monumental form of the Holy Sepulchre, the site of Christ's Resurrection and Christendom's most hallowed shrine, with which Christians who could not make the journey to Jerusalem could associate themselves *in absentia.*One may also postulate a symbolic expression of Christ's birthplace in a grotto that could be read as a prefiguration of the Entombment and Resurrection. The rock-cut church came therefore to represent the great mystery central to Christian belief of the birth, death, and resurrection of Christ. It is possible to detect in this Christian fascination with caves a debt to Oriental (particularly Zoroastrian) cosmology which saw in grottoes places that were "proper to genesis and departure from genesis", and according to whose mythology Mithras was born miraculously from a rock in a cave.

The first great centre for the diffusion of Christian troglodytic architecture was the Nile Valley where an ascetic, and often anchoritic, quality of early Christianity received inspiration from the Desert Fathers who fled civilization to set up monastic communities in the 'huge silence', *silentium ingens, quies magna,* of the African desert.Caves, both natural and man-made, and, when available sepulchers and cemeteries became in this way desirable sites for hermitages. The missionary activities of Coptic, Egyptian, and Syrian monks popularized the practice in Ethiopia,and all over Asia Minor from where it was adopted by the later Roman Empire, and, more especially, in those regions dominated by Greek Christianity and their border (and border-influenced) zones.

In Western Europe the two area of major proliferation were Sicily and the heel of the Italian peninsula, both of which were provinces of the Byzantine Empire. Vasiliev has shown how during the Iconoclastic crises of 726 – 843 A.D., a huge number of monks, perhaps as many as 50,000, fled persecution within the Empire and sought asylum in Italy.Many found refuge in Rome, where the Popes did not admit Byzantine control and were anxious to stress their disapproval of the heretical attitude of the eastern emperors, but the majority seem to have preferred the desolate South Italian countryside where the rock-cut churches bear striking similarities to the rock-cut monasteries of Cappadocia.There was another diaspora of monks into the central Mediterranean in 1071, after the battle Manzikert, when some of the monks presumably found their way to Sicily, and some might have touched at Malta.

The date of Malta's rock-cut churches cannot be securely documented, but in the light of the available evidence the early post-Muslim period seems best indicated. This does not exclude the existence of pre-Muslim establishments, particularly in association with hypogea and other cemeterial sites.The fact remains, nonetheless, that iconographical and architectural considerations seem to anchor the great majority of Maltese troglodytic churches in the late Middle Ages. This would make them coeval to most of the rock-cut churches in the Sicilian and South Italian countryside to which they have a close artistic and liturgical affinity. It is their relationship to the Christianisation of Maltese Muslims by Sicilian-Greek monastic communities who might have used them as nuclei of evangelization that remains to be ascertained.

## Interpreting the Toponyms

In addition to Abbatija tad-Dejr, Wettinger has noted the following other *dejr* toponyms:

| | | |
|---|---|---|
| 1. Dejr Baqqar | 2. Bieb id-Dejr | 3. Dejr il- Bużbież |
| 4. Dejr Deru | 5. Dejr Ħandun | 6. Dejr il-Ħmir |
| 7. Dejr l-Imara | 8. San Ġorġ ta' Dejr Magħlaq | 9. Dejr is-Safsaf |
| 10.Dejr iż-Żara | 11. Dejr is-Saf | 12.Dejr il-Bniet |
| | 13.San Ġwann tad-Dejr | |

A *Conttrata ta Deier Birzigrilla* is in addition mentioned in the 1575 Apostolic Vistation Report of Mgr. Pietro Dusina,but since it was apparently located at Rabat, not far from Għarxiem, it is probable that it formed part of the same territory as Abbatija tad-Dejr San Ġwann tad-Dejr (*Sancti Johannis de lu deyr*) which is mentioned as an *ecclesia,* in 1500 deed of Notary J. Sabbara, was, possibly in the same district, but its exactly locality is unknown. This toponym shares with San Ġorġ ta' Dejr Magħlaq (*Sancti Georgii di deyr mihallac*) the distinction of being associated with a

Christian saint. In both cases the toponym presumably got its name from a church that stood in the district. San Gorg ta' Dejr il-Maghaq was noted by Wettinger in a deed of 1494, which does not, however, indicated its location. He interpreted the name as 'Dejr of the Enclosed Area', and suggested a site in the SE of Malta, possibly at Birzebbuga (where a church of St. George is documented in 1575) or, perhaps, in the nearby anchorages of Marsaxlokk and Marsascala which both have a place called Il-Magħlaq.There is, nonetheless, a probability that the site can be identified with a *territorium di deyr limallac*, mentioned in a document of 1500 which defines the parish boundaries of the village of Siggiewi.Since the parish of Siggiewi had two churches with such a dedication to St. George, it may be possible to narrow the quest for the toponym to either of two possible localities.

One is the Ġebel Ciantar district at Ta' Żuta, near Fawwara, overlooking the precipitous cliffs of the west coast. The place is of archaeological interest on account of a late Roman site whose remains were at an unknown period reutilized by a Christian community who adapted a rock-cut columbarium into a church whose dedication to St. George can be documented to 1436.The topography of the place made it a likely place for a hermitage, and there are in the area an abundant fresh water spring, and several large caves that were inhabited until recent times.The other site is Wied il-Maghlaq, a lonely and desolate ravine close to the Għar Lapsi road. A church of St. George is documented there in 1575 when it was in an apparent state of dereliction.It was not an important church, but it is interesting to note that it had an association with the monks of San Nicoló l'Arena of Catania because it belonged to the endowment they received in 1363. The monks were, as a result bound to celebrate the feast of St. George with mass and vespers. Equally significant is the presence on the site of a small necropolis of Early Christian sepulchers.Their presence was, perhaps, a bigger attraction to anchoritic monasticism than the classical ruins at ta' Żuta, but the topography was less hospitable.

Dejr is-Saf, which is recorded as a *viridarium* in 1496, may derive its name from the Arabic personal name Saf. The site is identified with Tabrija (*della tabria sive di deyr isaf contrata*) in 1525, which presumably means that it was a district of this extensive royal fief, west of Siggiewi. Its approximate location in the neighbourhood of Bukett, at Ta' Xwejxa, near a church of the Virgin, is indicated in a 1548 document (*ta deir issaf viridarium in contrata S. Marie ta xeuxe*). A later 1557 document refers to the place as *sancta maria di deyr saf.* The church, which in 1575 celebrated the feast of the Purification of the Virgin, stood on high ground and was a prominent landmark visible from miles around. It was rebuilt in the seventeenth century, but is now a sad ruin. Its origins are unknown, but irrespective of its real significance, it is worth noting that the surrounding lands had by the time of the church's first mention become ecclesiastical property and an important part of the *mensa vescovile,* which fact was diligently noted in the 1575 report.

Dejr l-Imara presents a more interesting case study. It seems possible that it is similarly derived from a Semitic personal name, and a Basilius Limara *cives Melite* is mentioned in a 1324 document. His name may suggest a Greek-rite Christian of Muslim descent, but the word can have other meanings. Wettinger seems to be more inclined to translate it as "Dejr of the commanders" or the "admirals", and it should be emphasized that even if originating from a personal name, there is no justifiable reason why it should be associated a Muslim convert to Greek Christianity. The name is common and continues to be recorded in Malta until the early modern period.If the site does have a Christian significance it might prove more profitable to look for clues on the site itself. The topography of the place does not favour cave dwelling, and if there was a monastery, or anchoritic station, this was presumably built rather than rock-cut. Traces of

'Norman' buildings, supposedly including a church, and various rooms grouped round a courtyard, were diagnosed by Missione Archeologica Italiana a Malta, in the late 1960s, among the classical and paleoehristian remains at Tas-Silg, on the high ground which marks the start of the Delimara peninsula.

These scanty and highly problematic remains were interpreted as a possible monastic establishment. The dating was based on a scatter of glazed pottery with a hatching of brown lines on a creamy-white ground, which were thought to be Norman, but the typology seems to fit a wide arc of time between the ninth and fifteenth centuries, or even later. There was on the site a built trough-tomb that was vaguely dated to a post-1100 A.D. period.It is of course not improbable that a community of Greek-rite monks lived among the classical and Early Christian ruins of Tas-Silg. Dejr l-Imara may therefore be another case of a Greek-rite community rooting itself at a site where Christianity had known a vigorous early tradition interrupted by the Muslim invasion of 870 A.D. The Missione's archaeological interpretations must, however, be treated with caution.

Dejr il-Ħmir seems to present an analogous case. The topomym can likewise be associated a Muslim personal name (*Humir*), but it can also be interpreted as "Dejr of the donkeys". Its first known mention is in a deed of 1500 where it is located in a place called Nadur Għajxa, in the district of *rahal antun* (Hlantun).This late medieval settlement, which had been deserted by the first three decades of the 15th century,was named after a church of St. Anthony the Abbot,whose remains, consisting of a wall built of small, square ashlar blocks of the type used in late medieval buildings, could still be identified in 1970 when I took a measured drawing.

The church may already have been deconsecrated by 1575 and does not seem to be mentioned in the Dusina report of that year.Like Tas-Silġ, the place has notable archaeological significance, but its monuments are still largely unstudied. They include at least two late Roman round towers, namely Ta' Gawhar, and Ta' Torrijiet,and, at least, five paleochristian hypogea, besides a number of isolated rock-tombs. Among them the Tal-Liebru Hypogeum is worthy of particular attention on account of its carvings of several cross monograms some of which may, in fact, be late medieval rather than paleochristian.

Dejr iż-Żara should presumably be identified with Dar iż-Żara, at Ta' Qali, at the foot of the Saqqajja plateau, where a church of the Nativity of the Virgin, was reportedly built in 1431 on a preband of the Chapter of the Cathedral. A 1571 document which describes the site as *terri in contrata ta salib ta San Jacobo,*suggests the existence of a second church in the area.

Dejr il-Bniet, which can mean either "Benet's Dejr", or, more improbably, "Dejr of the girls", was the name of Crown fief that is first reported as a *viridarium* in 1351.The site borders on the late medieval settlements of Tartarni and Dingli whose church of S. Dominica was a *cappella,* or parish church, in 1436.The dedication is of interest because of its South Italian and Sicilian Greek-Christian associations. Dominica is the Latinised version of the Greek *Cyriaca,* a martyr of the Diocletian persecution who enjoyed a cult in the city of Tropea, in the Calabria, where her relics were translated at an unknown period in the Early Middle Ages. As in the case of Cataldus, and Philip of Aggira, it is probable that her cult reached Malta with the Normans.

Dejr Baqqar seems to have been located close to Dejr is-Saf in the fertile Girgenti Valley, no far from the Crown fief of Tabrija and Il-Wied ta' l-Isqof. A field of that name at the foot of Tal-Għolja Hill, at Siġġiewi, presumably indicated its approximate location, while an orchard, which in 1506, was known as *ta beb Jdeir,* could have marked some sort of landmark on the site. Situated in a sheltered, eastward-facing valley, with a good supply of fresh water, it had all the makings of an ideal setting for a community of hermit monks. No archaeological remains are today visible, but Abela mentions *vestigi di grossissime pietre e anticaglie.* The name could have derived from the Arabic personal name *Bakr,* but can also mean "Dejr of the cows".

Dejr Ħandun (or Ħandul), on the high plateau to the north of Dingli, was renowned for its fresh water springs that had been tapped for water supply since antiquity. The site, first mentioned in 1399, is presumably the same as Djar Ħandul, which was the site of vineyard in 1542. No church has been noted in the area, and, in spite of the fact that the likely translation of the name is "Ħandul's monastic-type building", there is nothing to suggest that the site had a religious significance.

Dejr Deru may, perhaps have acquired its name from a lentistic shrub that grew in the neighbourhood, although a derivation from a personal name is also possible. The site is unlocated. Godfrey Wettinger mentions a number of rural districts called Ta' Deru,but it is not possible to identify any of them with it. The most tempting, albeit arbitrary, is a field at Bubaqra where a church dedicated to the Eastern saint, Cyrus (San Ċir) had an apse mural of a Blessing Christ in the Siculo-Byzantinesque Pantocrator tradition.

Dejr il-Busbież, and Dejr is-Safsaf, may also have obtained their name from the characteristic vegetation of their location, the fennel shrub in one case, and the osier willow in the other. The former seems to be an alternative name for Wied il-Busbiez a fertile valley to the NW. of Rabat. The site, first mentioned in 1556,has all necessary amenities for a hermitage, but no Christian associations, have been reported from the area. Dejr is-Safsaf is, on the other hand, an unlocated district first mentioned as a *contrata* in 1467. An area called Ta' Safsaf, which in 1495 was a *territorium,* at Wied Ta' Bufula, in the district of Wardija, at St. Paul's Bay, might, possibly, have been the same site, but there is no way of ascertaining. The remains of "ancient" buildings were noted there at the turn of the seventeenth century, together with three churches of unknown antiquity with respective dedications to St.

John, St. Simon the Apostle, and St. Nicholas. That of St. John, known as *ta' Chereb* ('Of the Ruins') was thought to mark the place where St. Paul had baptized his shipmates after the shipwreck, as well as the site of Publius's country villa. This tradition could have been a modern fabrication, but it is also possible that it stemmed from the distant recollections of a Christian activity in the area which centred round the presence of Greek-rite monks.

### The *Raheb* Toponyms

Another possible clue to Greek-rite monasticism in early post-Muslim Malta may, perhaps, be preserved in a second set of toponyms that center around the Semitic word *raheb* (monk), or its derivatives. Wettinger has argued that the word referred to Western mendicant friars, notably Augustinians. The Romance word *patri*, was (and still is), however, in much more common usage, and it is possible that *raheb,* which is now virtually obsolete, qualified another type of monk, such as a one belonging to the

Greek-rite. It should be emphasized, however, that this is a hypothesis that still needs to be buttressed by scientific investigation, and it could also have been the case that in its late medieval context *raheb* meant all types of monks.

An eloquent *raħeb-* toponym is Bir ir-Rieħbu ('the Monk's Well) which refers to a site in close proximity to Abbatija tad-Dejr, at Rabat, thereby enforcing arguments for a monastic establishment there. The name, which is still in current use, was first mentioned as a *galca,* or field, in a deed of 1519. L-Irqajjaq tar-Raheb ('the Fields of the Monk') which was the name of an area, near the church of S. Lorenzo *tal gemune,* at Ta' Għolja, Siġġiewi, is also of interest for its possible associations with the nearby Dejr Baqqar, while a *clausura* called Ġnien tar-Rħieb, noted at Wied Qannotta, near Wardija, in 1611, may, perhaps, be an added argument, to the location in the area of Dejr is-Safsaf.

Raħeb place-names do not seem to be widely diffused. There was an un-located alley called Tar-Raħeb, in 1496, while two fields at Lija and Mrieħel respectively were known by that name in 1533 and 1539. The Mrieħel field was, perhaps identical with a *clausura* 'Ta' Raħba' which is recorded there in 1536. The name Raħba (*ta' raħibe*) was also borne by three strips of land at Marsalforn, on Gozo in 1496; by a field at Ħaż-Żebbug, in 1500; by a chantry lane at Tarxien, in 1536, and by an ecclesiastical benefice of undisclosed locality, in 1532.There was also, on Gozo, in 1564, a Wied ir-Raheb,apparently in the neighbourhood of the desolate Kap San Dimitri, while in Malta, an Andar ir-Raħeb ('The Threshing Floor of the Monk') is recorded, in the area of Fiddien, in 1621.

The most intriguing toponym, is however, Ras ir-Raħeb ('The Headland of the Monk'), on the remote NW corner of the Rabat-Dingli plateau. The place has archaeological interest and there are the remains of a Late Roman establishment, possibly a sanctuary.In

1647, Abela suggested that the area got its name from a peculiar rock formation that vaguely resembled the figure of a monk, but it is equally possible that the name stemmed from the recollection of a community of hermit monks who squatted among the ruins. The place has been unsatisfactorily excavated and published.

A valuable piece of evidence which was overlooked, is a large worked stone with present measurements of 111 x 65.5 x 0.35 cm, that lies partially in a shallow basin, bordered by beautifully squared stone blocks, at the back of one of the two megaliths which mark the site. It has a moulded base and chamfered edges and looks suspiciously like an altar-top, or perhaps, a tombstone. Its age and real purpose cannot possibly be ascertained, and it ought to be said that no demonstrably medieval sherds have so far been identified in the area which abounds in fragments of fine Roman red ware. Important testimonies may have been destroyed during the unhappy excavations of

1961-62, and the true history of the site will probably never be known. The toponomy of the place which, in addition to Ras ir-Raħeb, was also called Ras il-Knejjes ('The Headland of the Churches'), implying some sort of ecclesiastical connections, is, however, significant.

## The Evidence of the Built Churches

Although this study is concerned with rock-cult churches, it should be emphasized that hints of Greek and Oriental Christianity can also be found in the built churches of period. This is above all the case of the countryside churches which normally owed only a very superficial debt to the ecclesiastical architecture of the Latin West. There is, it is here argued, a close relationship between them and their rock-cut counterparts, and they seem likewise to be related to the earliest, post-Muslim native Christian communities. San Cir at Bubaqra,with its Siculo-Byzantinesque apse mural, was presumably not an isolated case, and it is significant that most of their dedications were to eastern saints or devotions. Architecturally they were uninspiring edifices. Constructed entirely of stone, they were plain one-cell buildings of severe box-like proportions. Roofing was by a system of stone slabs carried on the backs of transverse arches that rested on wall piers and divided the internal space into a regular sequence of bays that were lined with low stone benches. At the east end there was often a cylindrical apse, but the altar sometimes rested against a plain wall.

This typology of stone architecture, which originated in Arabia, and finds a close parallel in the early Christian churches of the Hauran in Syria, reached the western Mediterranean in the course of the Early Middle Ages as a result of the several migration waves of Middle Eastern monks. In 1993 I argued that it might have been introduced in Malta in sub-Saracenic times, by Sicilian Greek-rite monks.Direct evidence is lacking, but it should be pointed out that in Eastern Sicily, churches with similar ground plans and construction methods, had close connections with Basilian coenobitic monasticism. One church in particular, San Barnaba in Valderice, had the same structural idiosyncrasies. Others though largely analogous have different roofs which in their present state are either barrel-vaulted or made of timber. The original roofs were in most cases rebuilt in the early modern period.

# Attractions

## Birgu

Birgu, the ancient maritime city that is proud of its title 'Citta Vittoriosa', is packed with history, artistic and architectural splendour. As you wander down its fascinating winding streets, layers of different cultures unfold, stretching from the Roman period, to the medieval overlords in the strong castle at fort St Angelo, to the glorious knights' period when Birgu, the home of the mighty Order of St John was the pride of Europe after its victory in the bitter Great Siege of 1565, now immortalised by best-selling historical novels like "The Sword and the Scimitar" by David Ball, "Blood Rock" by James Jackson and "The Religion" by Tim Willocks.

Strolling along this walled city surrounded by mighty fortifications, memories of its past haunt the visitor, though the present city is full of life, thanks to its magnificent churches, band clubs, bars, taverns and top restaurants set among the residences of a proud but humble city.

Birgu's 'Castrum Maris' or Castle by the Sea, was for a time the centre of Maltese civil, religious and social life, especially during the Knights' period when important institutions in Birgu dominated Maltese society. These included the old hospital of the Order built in 1534, now the residence of the cloistered nuns of St Benedict. The rebuilt Church of the Dominicans, the Conventual Church of St Lawrence, as well as the unique Inquisitors' Palace are all worth visiting, especially as the Oratory of St. Lawrence proudly holds the hat and sword of Jean de Vallette, the heroic Grand Master who led the Knights of St. John to victory during the Great Siege. The Inquisitor's Palace has been superbly restored and is now a museum of the

Inquisition in Malta and religious tradition. The knights' palaces or 'Auberges', added to the grandeur of Birgu, particularly the Auberge d' Angleterre and the Auberge de France, presently the seat of the Birgu Local Council. Thought to have been designed and embellished by the great medieval architect Bartolomeo Genga, this magnificent Auberge has now been restored to its former grandeur.

Birgu's characteristic town square is the hub of the town and wonderful spot to linger over a coffee, while the unique setting of the restored waterfront has attracted some of the best restaurants where diners can enjoy the view of the yacht marina set against the backdrop of Senglea across the creek. The ' Marina Grande' as the Knights called it, was a famous shipyard dating back to the Middle Ages. With the coming of the Knights in 1530 maritime activities increased, and in fact in the 17$^{th}$ century it was considered one of the finest shipyards in the Mediterranean. This made it the ideal spot for Malta's Maritime Museum located in the converted Naval Bakery and displaying a rich collection of items related to Malta's sea-faring past.

Birgu's restoration efforts are now focused on its fascinating Collachio – the area that had been reserved for the sole use of the knights - and the bastion known as the Post of Castille which is shown in frescoes of the magnificent Sala del Gran Consiglio at the President's Palace in Valletta. The massive restoration of Fort St Angelo at the tip of the Birgu promontory marks a new era for this ancient city and its surroundings.

The miraculous rebirth of Birgu can only be appreciated if one knows of the destruction that the Three Cities – Birgu, Bormla and Senglea suffered during the Second World War (1939-1945). Reduced to a rubble wasteland of bombed houses, churches and palaces, it seemed impossible that the area could ever recover.

In spite of this terrible time, Birgu has lived up to its proud title of Citta Vittoriosa and has risen from its ashes to become once again a city that draws people to its vibrant shores.

## Dingli

Dingli is one of the most beautiful Maltese villages, perched on the most spectacular cliffs on the island. It is also blessed with well-watered fields fed by freshwater streams that percolate above the clay layer making it one of the few Maltese settlements that is still characterised by rural activities all year round.

Dingli's rural character led to the development of one of the most interesting and professional sustainability projects in Malta. The Dingli Sustainable Development Strategy – a venture that allowed the Local Council to tap EU funds for sustainable development in rural areas and publish a strategy that is currenly being implemented.

The first part of the Heritage Trail that forms the backbone of the sustainability project takes the visitor to a number of important historical and environmental landmarks.

The statue of Francis Ebejer, Malta's leading playwright and writer greets the visitors' eyes as they alight off the local bus. Ebejer is one of the most distinguished Maltese citizens and walking towards the Parish Church of St. Mary reveals the town's centre of devotion. The Church's belfries provide the highest place in Malta and offer spectacular views of the surroundings to visitors.

The Heritage Trail leads the visitor to a number of chapels, all of which have their own history and traditions. The same area also has a number of bars where a visitor can sample traditional pastizzi and have a home-made cup of tea or a glass of wine.

Walking beyond St. Mary's Parish Church visitors arrive at Dingli Cliffs, some of which are over 200 metres high and offer an incomparable panorama of the small islet of Filfla, especially during sunset!

St. Mary Magdalene Chapel which was rebuilt on the cliff edge in 1646 is a historic attraction. Perched above cliffside fields, it shows the problems Maltese farmers have to face when tilling the windswept land.

Visitors wanting more information on the attractions of Dingli and its surroundings, and at the same time sample some Maltese cuisine, should visit the new Interpretation Centre, which is promising to be the inofficial information office on Dingli and its attractions.

Back to the other side of Dingli, just before entering the town proper is one of the most interesting places that has also been recently rehabilitated. This is the freshwater spring locally known as L-Għajn tal-Ħassellin or the washers' stream, where housewives used to gather to do their laundry. The path leading to one of the few permanent streams that flows during summer is heavily festooned with mulberry treesand further down, maidenhair ferns (Tursin il-Bir). It is also an area steeped in myth and tradition and forms an important landmark on the Heritage Trail.

For those visitors interested in the biodiversity of the area, the cliffsides offer excellent bird-watching views, but to experience the beauty of a Maltese valley, a visit to Wied Ħażrun is a must.

The valley is important for two reasons. Freshwater flows all year round, irrigatingsome of the oldest cultivable fields on the island as well asa very rare stand of relict Holm Oaks, whose ancestors date back to Neolithic times. The area also contains swathes of garigue and maquis that are festooned with plants and flowers in Spring.

These are only some of the highlights of what Dingli offers. The Heritage Trail provides detailed information and directions on all the sights described and more.

**Winter flowers on the windswept cliffs of Dingli**

The Dingli Cliffs in the west of Malta rise over 800 feet above sea level and contain the highest points on the island. Due to their height and exposure the cliffs usually bear the brunt of the prevailing north-west wind, the *Majjistral,* which generally tends to be a cruelly cold wind in winter and a welcome cool one in summer.

This evening, I managed a quick 60 minute dash to the cliffs in search of some early flowering species before the spring riot of wild flowers and was rewarded with a beautiful variety of species, including three new ones that I had never managed to observe before.

The first floral species I chanced upon was the wild clary sage (*Salvia verbenaca*) known as *salvja selvaġġa* in Maltese. Although it is classified as a separate species, it is obviously a wild "cousin" of the domestic sage grown in our gardens. This was my first ever observation of this tiny but beautiful plant whose leaf and flower are used to enhance salads in nearby Italy.

Walking along the uneven *karst* surface of the *garigue,* I passed numerous clumps of the very common

Mediterranean heather (*Erica multiflora),* known as *erika* in Maltese. The pale pink, dark tipped floral clusters of this low bushy plant provide a beautiful spectacle in the relatively bleak wintry landscape. This richly flowering plant is reputed to be very attractive to honey bees.

Crossing the coastal road to a stretch of garigue which was once an enclosed field which has since lost most of its soil cover, I came across my first ever experience of the delicate white flowers of the Mediterranean hartwort (*Tordylium apulum),* known in Maltese as the *haxixet it-trieraq*. This plant is related to the carrot family and although common I had never managed to notice it in my countryside forays. The ground in the degenerated field was teeming with these beautiful specimens which are best enjoyed close-up as in the picture above.

My big surprise of the day came in the form of a solitary Brown orchid (*Ophrys fusca),* known in Maltese by the highly descriptive if not demeaning name of *dubbiena* or fly due to its similarity to the winged pest. Maltese orchids are not huge in size and tend to be very elusive to the point of being missed by most. But once you adjust your eyesight to the relevant scale you start seeing them where there was nothing before. Although the brown orchid is apparently a relatively common species, this was my first ever observation of its kind: a joyful experience reminiscent of the reaction of a collector who has just added a rare item to his collection! My search for other specimens of this orchid were fruitless so I consider myself very lucky to have witnessed this tiny but beautiful plant when I could have just as easily bypassed it.

The last floral species I witnessed on this short sojourn to the cliffs was another type of orchid, of which there were numerous specimens scattered around the landscape. This orchid, which is either the Conical or Milky orchid (due to their almost perfect similarity) is known in Maltese as the *orkida tat-tikek* or the spotted orchid due to its beautiful pattern of pink dots on the delicate white petals. Of all the photos of the different specimens I captured on this trip, my favourite is the one above with the full cluster of flowers contrasting against the backdrop of a lichen encrusted rock.

So all in all quite a rich harvest of beautiful and natural works of art at a time of the year when most of our northern neighbours are still weeks away from even dreaming of flowers re-emerging from their cold and desolate landscapes.

# Isla (Senglea)

Isla (or Senglea), is the smallest of the Three Cities in Cottonera. This town is situated on a peninsula protruding into the Grand Harbour, facing the charming walled city of Valletta. The name of 'Isla' is derived from the Italian word '*isola*' (island), which describes how the peninsula is nearly cut off from land by Mill Hill and St Julian's Hill.

This locality is truly one of the jewels of the Maltese Islands, being also one of the oldest cities dating back to the 16th century. This maritime city not only boasts of a rich heritage but also contains many structures built by the Knights themselves, making it one of the heaviest fortified areas on the Island. It is indeed a gem enclosed by spectacular bastions, overlooking stunning views and still guarding the Grand Harbour as it did centuries ago.

Going for a stroll to *Ġnien il-Gardjola* (the look-out garden) at the tip of Senglea Point, one can enjoy a blend of history and the Mediterranean. From the lonely caper tree clinging to the bastions, to the ancient fig trees scattered haphazardly, it seems that the island's gentle climate has in time fused with the city itself. Looking down towards the calm waves of the harbour, one can still see the beating heart of the cities - the dockyard which was set up by the Knights and later developed further by the British as a naval shipyard.

Isla reflects also Malta's religious heritage with many niches holding revered statues of patron saints and an astounding basilica dedicated to Our Lady of Victories. The striking images of the elderly praying in these old churches show the depth of Malta's religious beliefs.

This city is more than a place adorned with character and heritage. Life flows through its narrow streets amongst its aged buildings. Many activities take place within the city, amongst which the popular *Regattas* (traditional boat races) which take place on the waters of the Grand Harbour twice a year- on the 31st March and 8th September, with Isla being one of the major contenders. September the 8th heralds Isla's biggest celebrations with the city *festa* where the town is lavishly decorated and lit by hundreds of light bulbs and spectacular fireworks. More recently, another event has been added to the local calendar- the *Martime Senglea Festival* (September) which is truly a celebration of the local culture, history and its relationship with the sea.

Really and truly however, no word can describe Isla. Only by visiting such a small distinctive place, nestled in the heart of the Grand Harbour can one really savour its true charm.

**Isla at a glance**

Located: Eastern side of the Maltese Islands, into the Grand Harbour

<u>Main attractions</u>
Gardjola Gardens
Senglea Point (swimming)
Senglea Promenade
Macina (Sheer Bastion)
Villa Sirena
Senglea Bastions
Fort St. Michael
Basilica of Our Lady of Victories
Church of St. Philip (Porto Salvo)
St. Julian's Chapel

<u>Main events</u>
March/ April

- ✓ 31st Regatta Races
- ✓ Good Friday and Easter Sunday Processions

May

- ✓ 8thSenglea Day

September

- ✓ 8th Our Lady of Victory Feast
- ✓ 8th Regatta Races
- ✓ Maritime Senglea Festival

# Ta' Sannat

Located in the south of Gozo, Ta' Sannat is a terraced village stretching from the nearby village of Munxar to the small secluded bay of Mġarr ix-Xini. Terraced fields fill the valleys to the east of the village and the previous quarry sites renowned for their good globigerina stone that employed most of the locals from ancient times until recently.

### Earliest inhabitants

Already in prehistoric times, Sannat's location was so suitable for settlement that a prehistoric community set up at Ta' Ċenċ. Structural remains dating from the Mġarr phase (3,800-3,600 B.C.) and known as *Ta' l-*

*Imramma* still survive to this day, revealing these people's religious beliefs and their worship practices.

The same plateau was still occupied in the earliest stages of the Bronze Age (2,400 - 1,500 B.C.) when dolmens were built on the Ta' Ċenċ plateau possibly marking burial sites. Other forms of prehistoric activity are evident from the cart-ruts scattered all over the plateau.

In Phoenician, Punic and Roman times, agriculture thrived around nearby Mġarr ix-Xini Valley. Olives and grapes produced oil and wine for local use and export. The farmers working the terraced fields are likely to have lived in the same area where they also erected a small shrine at Għar ix-Xiħ overlooking Mġarr ix-Xini Bay, which served as a small harbour from where they could export their surplus products. Recent archaeological studies in the area are already yielding interesting results, dating back human activity there as early as the 6th century B.C.

## Sannat becomes a parish

To safeguard their agricultural produce, the Sannat farmers erected towers such as the *Tal-Ħofra* tower near the village main square and *Ta' Ġjammajr* overlooking Tal-Gruwa. A few chapels characterised this typically Gozitan rural landscape and one of them – dedicated to St Margaret of Antioch, an early 4th century A.D. martyr – became the first parish church when the village became a parish on 28th April 1688. The parish priest used to live in a fine town-house in one of the streets behind the church until he moved to the current residence next to the present church.

Until it reached its present form, the church was altered several times. The chapel of St Margaret already existed in 1615 but soon after it became a parish it was felt to be too small for the spiritual needs of its growing parish so it was enlarged in 1718 and again during the second half of the 19th century, bringing the church to its present form. These alterations were concluded with the building of the dome in 1910.

**Village life down to present times**

The inhabitants of Sannat have always shared the same fate as the rest of the Gozitans, suffering famines or shortage of employment along with the rest, and were not spared any plagues hitting the island from time to time like the cholera epidemic of 1837 or that of 1865. Wars left their mark too. The village was, in fact, to suffer most during World War II when it had the largest number of casualties in Gozo, particularly during a very severe attack on 10th October 1942.

After the war, many young villagers had to seek work abroad, particularly in Australia, America, and Canada. In this way, they were also able to support their families whom they often left behind them. Many of them prospered and were able to return back and re-settle here. But the economy had changed - few relied any longer on agriculture or quarrying for their living and had to enter other sectors, but they do not fare any worse than other Gozitans.

## Mdina Attractions

Malta's old capital, the Silent City, *Ċitta' Notabile*, some of the names Mdina has been given during its amazing history which spans thousands of years but also different empires and civilisations.

It is not yet clear whether the Temple Builders were present on the hilltop now occupied by Mdina but recent archaeological excavations have revealed remains from the Bronze Age. Through ancient written sources we know that the city was known as Melite and was occupied by the Carthaginians. Phoenician tombs have been widely found in areas surrounding Mdina, especially on the next hilltop at Mtarfa. The Romans conquered Malta from the Carthaginians in 218 BC.

Back then Mdina was much larger, its walls enclosing an extensive area of Rabat. In fact part of the ancient

Roman ditch is located behind the main church in Rabat while a Roman country villa, the Domus Romana and Roman Christian catcombs have been located just beyond the current walls of Mdina. It is highly likely that the city was reduced in size during the time of the Byzantines. The latter were defeated in battle by the Arab forces who changed the name of the city to the one by which it is still known, Mdina.

After the Normans conquered the Maltese Islands back into the Christian fold in 1090 AD, various noble families settled in Mdina however Malta's destiny was far from settled. The Maltese Islands passed to the German Hohenstaufen dynastywhich was defeated by the Angevins from France. The Angevins were later defeated in the Battle of Malta by the crown of Aragon. The Maltese noble families gained particular importance after a Royal Charter dated 20th June 1482 from King Alfonso V confirmed the right of the Maltese to excercise local power over the islands.This gave the Maltese Islands a degree of independence, setting up a local government, the *Universita'* and the *Consiglio Popolare*, or local Council, which could deliberate local affairs but had no legislative power.

When the Knights of St John arrived, this self-governing power was lost, which caused a great deal of resentment among the the nobles; in fact they sent a representative to protest to Viceroy of Sicily. Since Mdina's fortifications were quite inadequate and the Knights needed to be close to their gallies in harbour, they opted to defuse the situation by makingBirgu their base, leaving the nobles to their splendid isolation in Mdina. It was only after the highly destructive earthquake of 1693 that the knights of St John moved in and left their imprint through the remodelling of Mdina.

The Mdina gate was built under the patronage of Grandmaster de Vilhena of the Order of St John in 1724. Mdina's fortifications had been been ignored for a long period of time but after the great 1693 earthquake, Manoel de Vilhena took the opportunity to imprint the Order's image on Mdina, commissioning French Engineer Charles Francois de Mondion to remodel the old city and its defenses.

On the left hand side of the gate in the wall there are the remains of the older drawbridge gate dating to Mdina's Arab age. This gate led to a labyrinthine entrance to the old city: all those who entered had to zig-zag through a narrow passage before entering the citadel, which would allow the defenders to ambush invaders if they managed to penetrate past the gate.

De Redin Bastion rises out of the deep moat beneath the bridge. This bastion system forms part of Malta's fortifications which were among the most advanced of their day as in addition to having their own resident European engineer, the Knights would regularly call to Malta leading European fortifications experts to advise on the strengthening of the fortifications. At the back of the main gate there is a lunette sculpted in high relief shows the three patron saints of the city: Saint. Publius, Saint. Paul and Saint Agatha. There are also the arms of the city and of the Inguanez family. The Inguanez were for many years the Governors of Mdina.

The Vilhena Palace also known as the Magisterial Palace was constructed by Grandmaster de Vilhena in 1722 on the site of the medieval Arab entrance into Mdina which once housed the medieval local government of the *Universita'*. The design of the building is one of the best works by the Order's French resident engineer, de Mondion and hence, in 1726 this Mdina palace was built in the Parisian Baroque style. the Vilhena Palace also served as a hospital during the 1847 cholera outbreak and continued to serve as a hospital for tuberculosis patients until the early 20th century.

Since 1973 the Palazzo became the National Museum of Natural History, today managed by Heritage Malta. This life and earth sciences museum is the national repository of biological specimens presenting themes such as human evolution, insects, birds and habitats and marine ecosystems.

Opposite this at St. Publiuis Square the *Torre dello Standardo* signal tower was built in the early 18th century replacing an older 16th century tower. The arms of De Vilhena and the city of Mdina were put on the tower after its remodelling. A signal fire on this tower would send a warning to a chain of towers in the surrounding towns and villages, warning the population that enemy corsairs were sighted approaching Malta.

At *Misraħ il-Kunsill* there is the Xara Palace, currently a hotel, which dates from thefifteenth century. Adjoining Xara Palace you can witness Herald's Loggia where the Town Herald use to read the proclamations issued by the *Universita'*, that used to manage the island's local affairs in the fifteenth century. Opposite the Xara Palace the facade of the Corte Capitanale, which forms part of the Vilhena Palace looks down on the square. This building used to house the Courts of Justice, its statues of Mars, the God of war, and Justice, reminding the population that  the Order would not hesitate to impose order through justice or the sword. Today the Corte Capitanale houses the Local Council of Mdina.

The chapel of St Agatha dates back to 1410 but in 1693 it was also damaged during during the earthquake. The chapel was rebuilt on the design of Lorenzo Gafa and opened in the presence of Grand Master Adrien de Wignacourt  in 1695. Commemarative medals were buried in the masonry to mark the event. The nunnery of St Benedict was founded in the fifteenth century in the location of a previous hospital of St. Peter. The monastery has undergone many modifications during the years but the architecture is predominantly Baroque.

The present imposing portal in *Triq Villegaignon* is a 19th century creation however various artefacts have been unearthed from the gardens of Casa Inguanez, which are largely attributed to the Roman Melite period. The Inguanez are Malta's oldest aristocratic family, parts of the Palazzo dating back to the 14th century. Casa Testaferrata, the residence of the

Marquis of St Vincent Ferreri. He was another member of the Maltese nobility who was given this title in 1716 by King Philip V of Spain.

The *Banca Giuratale* was built in 1730 as the new 'home' of the *Universita'*. The portal on the top of the doorway is richly decorated with armour, arms and flags while trophy sculptures on each corner of the building are made up of symbols of the Knights' military power.

In the square next to the *Banca Giuratale* one finds the house used by the chief magistrate. Casa Gourgion stands on the upper left corner of the square, boasting a beautiful ceramic roundel. Next to it a Victorian neo-Gothic house dating to the British period, contrast strikingly with the rest of the buildings. The square is dominated by St. Paul's Cathedral, a baroque twin-belfried cathedral was rebuilt in 1702, after in 1693, the previous Romanesque Cathedral dating back to the 13th century, was badly damaged by a violent earthquake that wiped out much of Sicily. The new cathedral was designed by Lorenzo Gafa, a very well known Maltese architect who designed several churches around the Maltese Islands in Baroque style. This square was created when several streets and houses were cleared to create an open square in front of the cathedral appropriate to the size and splendour of the church.

The Archbishop Palace was constructed after the earthquake of 1693. However, Mdina had been the seat of the Bishop from the 16th century. The French General Vaubois dined here in 1798 as the guest of his conquered enemy. The Cathedral Museum is housed in an 18th century palace built as a diocesan seminary by Bishop Alpheran de Bussan and designed by Andrea belli. The museum collection includes *objets d'art*, Cathedral archives, archives of the Inquisition and those of the *old Universita*'.

From the bastions of Bastion Square one can view most of Malta, from Paola to Valletta, Sliema and Mosta with the very visible Rotunda church dome, said to be the third largest in the world. St Paul's Bay and Mtarfa are closest, Mtarfa being the nearest hill to the left which is thought to have been the burial place when Malta formed part of the Roman Empire.

Palazzo Falson dates from 1495 and was build by Admiral Falson. When the knights of St John arrived in Malta in 1530, Grandmaster Isle Adam was received in this house. On the outside of the facade of the building you can observe the beautiful double windows, divided by slender calonettes; they date from the 15th century Mdina Palazzo Falson which was bought by Captain Olof Frederick Gollcher in 1927.

The Carmelite Church and Convent is remembered for the important historical event of 1798. The revolt against the French was started when the French were about to auction the tapestries and other artifacts taken from this Church and the ringing of the Carmelite church bells are known to have signalled the start of the resistance. The present church was built in 1659 on design of Francesco Sammut, however Lorenzo Gafa is known to have been involved. The altar-piece of the 'Annunciation' was produced by Maltese artist Stefano Erradi.

The original Palazzo Santa Sofia was a one storey building, but in 1939 another floor was built imitating late medieval style. The ground floor was mostly used for stores, stables and the kitchen.On the side of Palazzo Santa Sophia in St Sophia Street you can witness a *siqifah.* The *'siqifah'* is an arched passageway tunnelled into massively built ground floors of buildings and leading into the courtyard or '*cortile domorum*' area, round which houses were normally built. In this case the*'siqifah'* opens into the narrow street thus bisecting the building into two areas.

St Roque Chapel was constructed in 1728 and is sometimes known as the chapel of *'Our Lady of the Light'*. St Roque was invoked especially in the times of diseases such as the plague. At that time St Roque's chapel was located near the entrance to the city but it was demolished during Vilhena's replanning of the city and relocated to its present location.

At the corner between Mesquita street and Gatto Murina street stands the the 14th century Gatto-Murina Palace. The double windows together with their scupltured hood moulds can be noticed. Mesquita Square contains also a number of 17th century houses. In this square you can notice that some houses have a *Muxrabija.*

St. Nicholas Chapel was built in 1550 and was rebuilt to the designs of Lorenzo Gafa in 1692. St Nicholas is a very popular saint in the eastern Orthodox religion and this part of Mdina was frequented by residents of Imdina hailing from Greece who were mostly occupied in humble occupations like garbage collection which was strictly regulated in order to avoid disease in the citadel.

Magazines Street is named because of the storehouses in the street that used to house weapons and ammunition. Once in Magazines street you will notice the ‘hole in the wall’, which is of recent construction. Through this tunnel you can see the old Valletta-Mdina railroad station built outside Mtarfa in 1890.

Greek or slave’s gate as it is known, was also built by Vilhena during the remodelling of Mdina in 1727. It seems that de Mondion did not order the demolition of the old gate but added a new Baroque skin onto it. The gate is called ‘Greeks’ gate’ due to the Greek community that lived in the southwest of the city in the 16th and 17th centuries. St. Paul is commemorated in the inscription on Greek’s gate

## Mdina Cathedral

According to tradition, St. Paul's Cathedral stands on the traditional site of the home of St Publius, father of the governor of the island at the time that St Paul was shipwrecked in Malta. St Paul is said to have healed Publius who converted toChristianity and went on to become the bishop of Malta and later of Athens. The

Cathedral of St. Paul was built from 1697 to 1702 to replace a Norman cathedral dating back to the 13th century which can be seen in two of Matteo Perez d'Aleccio's frescos in the Grand Masters' Palace in Valletta. Since plans to rebuild the cathedral were already in hand at the time of the earthquake, and within less than 10 years it was rebuilt, reaching completion in 1702.

Designed by architect Lorenzo Gafa, St. Paul's Cathedral is a fine structure whose façade impresses visitors as they emerge from Mdina's narrow streets. The cathedral's magnificent dome, painted a traditional deep red dominates the skyline. Lorenzo Gafa had already designed several churches in Malta and was at the height of his career when he was commissioned to rebuild Mdina's cathedral. The perfectly proportioned façade and the powerful dome (by far his boldest and arguably the finest in Malta) make this the most impressive of all his churches. The work took just five years to complete and the new cathedral caused a significant redesign of medieval Mdina's city centre as several streets and houses were cleared to create an open square in front of the cathedral appropriate to the size and splendour of the church.

The near-square facade is cleanly divided in three bays by the pilasters which are decorated in a Maltese variant of the Corinthian style. Bell towers stand at both corners of the façade which is also decorated by fine clocks. Accroding to legend, the clock on the left was purposely placed there to confuse the devil since it does not appear to tell the correct time. In reality it shows the date and month of the year. The clock on the right is the time-keeper and it strickes every 15 minutes. The plan is a Latin cross with a vaulted nave, two aisles and two small side chapels. The Cathedral has a light octagonal dome, with eight stone scrolls above a high drum leading up to a neat lantern.

The lavish interior of the cathedral is in many ways similar to the Cathedral of St. John in Valetta; though not quite as rich, it is still reminiscent of that church in the gilded carvings, the ornamental side chapels and the paintings that adorn the vault, apse and chapels. Many of the paintings and carvings illustrate scenes from the life of St Paul; the finest is Mattia Preti's monumental mural depicting the conversion of St. Paul decorating in between the apse and the main altar. This was one of the few treasures in the old church that survived the earthquake. Also surviving from the old church are the 15th-century Tuscan panel painting of the Madonna and Child; the baptismal font; the frescoes in the apse depicting St. Paul's shipwreck; and the old portal, made of carved Irish bog wood, which now serves as a door to the vestry. A marble-inlaid floor with tombstones carries the coats of arms and inscriptions of the bishops of Mdina and other members of the cathedral chapter. The dome's interior has been decorated by a succession of painters; today's decoration dates from the 1950s.

**Mdina Cathedral Museum**

Treasures salvaged from the original earthquake cathedral are now housed in a splendid baroque palace which once served as a Diocesan seminary. The collection of paintings, prints, woodcuts and old master drawings is the legacy of Count Saverio Marchese (1757 - 1833), a wealthy patron of the arts. Particularly fine among the works of art are the woodcuts by Durer, the engravings by Rembrandt and the 14th-century St Paul Polyptych which once adorned the high altar of the old cathedral. Here St Paul , enthroned in majesty, is surrounded by graphic depictions of episodes from his life. Among other museum exhibits are finely illustrated choir books, elaborate vestments, silver plate and a coin collection spanning over 2,000 years, including a complete set of Roman coins minted in Malta and Gozo. The old refectory of the seminary has been preserved, as has the charming 18th-century octagonal chapel.

**8 October 1703, the Consecration of the Cathedral of Mdina**

On October 8 of each year, in Malta, we celebrate the Dedication or Consecration of the Mother Church of the Archdiocese, the Cathedral of St Paul of Mdina. According to tradition, this was the site of the house of Publius, the prince of Malta who welcomed St Paul. For about 300 years, this church was the only large church on the island. Originally the titular was the Assumption but during the Arab rule period everything was destroyed.

During the Norman rule we find that the first churches were being built in 1127 and naturally within the three existing fortifications of Mdina, Saint Angelo and the fortification in Rabat, Gozo. We find in a document that in 1299 the church of the fortification of Mdina was dedicated to St Paul. The church erected during the Norman period was in Siculo-Norman style. The first idea to build the new cathedral dates to 1679 when the chapter, encouraged by Bishop Michael Hieronymus Molina (1678-1682) decided to replace the choir of the 13th century by a modern substitute in the

Baroque style. They appointed Lorenzo Gafa' to oversee the construction.

The 1693 Sicily earthquake was a powerful earthquake that struck parts of southern Italy, notably Sicily, Calabria and Malta on January 11, 1693 around 9 pm local time. The former Cathedral suffered considerable damage in the earthquake and was almost totally destroyed with most of the buildings of Mdina.

Bishop Davide Cocco Palmieri and the Cathedral Chapter decided to rebuild the church and the first stone was solemnly laid by the Bishop on May 1st, 1697. The building was on the design of Lorenzo Gafa' who had already thought of some plans even before the earthquake. It took five years to finish the present Cathedral built in the Baroque style. The new Cathedral was completed in 1702 a few months before the death of its inspired and famous architect Lorenzo Gafa' who died on the 16 February 1703 at the age of 64. Bishop Cocco Palmieri solemnly consecrated it on the 8th October 1703.

A Cathedral church is the mother of all the churches of the diocese. It is the seat of the Bishop of the whole diocese from where he teaches, governs and unites all the Catholic members of the church. The Cathedral of Mdina bears the title of 'Metropolitan' since the Bishop of Malta was raise to the dignity of Metropolitan Archbishop and head of the ecclesiastical province of Malta and Gozo in 1944.

## Palazzo Vilhena

The site of the Magisterial Palace has been occupied since prehistoric times when a bronze-age settlement existed here. In the 6th century BC the site formed part of a large walled Carthaginian town which was Romanized and known as *Melite*after 218BC. A Byzantine military establishment or *Kastron*, a Muslim fort and a Sicilian Chiaramonte castle existed here in Medieval times, with their ruins being converted to an elaborate crooked entrance designed to impede the entry of enemies into the old capital. Grand Master

Villiers de L'Isle Adam had also built a small palace here soon after the arrival of the Knights in Malta in 1530, however it remained very incomplete.

The Magisterial Palace at Mdina, is more commonly known as Palazzo Vilhena after Grand Master Antonio Manoel de Vilhena (1722-1736) who commissioned its building as part of his plan to restructure Medieval Mdina, ravaged by 1693 earthquake, rebuilding much of the Medieval former capital in the image of the Knights of St John who ruled the island at the time. The original building had served as the seat of the *Universita'*, or local Government. In the early 18th century, a new entrance to the city was constructed and the adjacent Magisterial Palace of Justice built just within the medieval walled city of Mdina at personal expense of the Portuguese Grand Master de Vilhena represents one of the most important and unique Baroque buildings in Malta. A bronze bust of the Grandmaster of the Order sits proudly above the main door and Vilhena's coat-of-arms are sculptured on the main gateway and inside the portico.

The Palace was designed in 1725 by the Parisian military engineer Charles Francois de Guion de Mondion who had been trained by the great Vauban and who had first came to Malta in 1715 as deputy head of a French military mission sent out by King Louis XIV to help the Knights upgrade their fortifications. Mondion's plan of the palace is based on an outer forecourt, which replaced the Mediaeval crooked entrance to the town, and an inner courtyard, which was inspired by the presence on the same site of an older courtyard forming part of the residence built by L'Isle Adam. Mondion's design for the palace's street facade based on a wall interrupted by an impressive portal and giant pilasters was inspired by late seventeenth century French palace architecture designed in the classical style of Versailles. The elliptical (flattened) arches that surround the courtyard on the two upper floors give the building a dramatic and theatrical quality, making this superb example of Baroque architecture, similar to other buildings designed by de Mondion in Malta such as Fort Manoel, the Calcara magazines and the Manoel theatre. Mondion's main problem was the sandwiched deep foundations of these earlier buildings, remains of which can still be seen in the palace courtyard, and weak bedrock which had repeatedly caused damage to the Mediaeval fortifications and continues to do so to this day.

Vilhena Palace also once housed the Mdina law courts, which explains why a number of cells can still be found inside. The palace's side façade, facing Xara Palace, is decorated with a statue portraying *'Justice'* which was not blindfolded, to give the message that justice is all-seeing and all-knowing.

During a cholera outbreak in 1837 the palace was turned into a temporary hospital and later used as a sanatorium for British troops. It was still being used as a tuberculosis hospital in the early 20$^{th}$ century. The palace suffered serious bomb damage during WWII and so even though it had been intended to be used as a museum as early as the 1960s, it only opened as a National Museum of Natural History in 1973.

Vilhena Palace is now contains several historically important collections, including more than 10,000 rock and mineral samples, 200 mammals and 200 fish species, 3,500 birds, birds' eggs and nests, as well as thousands of local and exotic shells and insects and a very impressive fossil collection.

## St. Agatha's Chapel

The chapel of St. Agatha in the ancient capital city of Mdina is of great historical interest dating back as it does to 1410. Originally built by the nobleman Francesco Gatt and his wife Donna Paola Castelli, the chapel was damaged during the great earthquake of 1693 and was remodelled and rebuilt in 1694 to a design of Lorenzo Gafa', the architect responsible for the Mdina Cathedral with its splendid baroque dome.

It was opened by the Bishop, Fra David Cocco-Palmieri in the presence of Grand Master Adrien de Wignacourt, a Frenchman, on the 26th June 1696. Commemorative medals were buried in the masonry to mark the event.

In 1551, Muslim forces under the command of Sinan Pasha landed in St. Paul's Bay and in what could have been a dress rehearsal for the Great Siege of 1565, camped in Mtarfa and laid siege to the capital then known as Notabile. When the supplies of the defenders were running low, the Vicar General, Don Giuseppe Manduca, was called to the Benedictine Abbey of Santa Scolastica then situated in Bastion Square (and now housed in Vittoriosa) to listen to a nun who claimed to have had a vision. The nun told the Vicar General that St. Agatha had appeared and had advised that Mass should be celebrated and that all soldier and civilians should walk in procession carrying her image which should be displayed on the bastions facing the enemy.

The Vicar General acted on this advice and the Bailiff Adomo, Governor of the city, together with the Knights of the Order of St. John and the Nobles and people of the city took part in a Service celebrated by the Bishop's Vicar. The Muslim forces said to have been impressed by the numerous defenders lifted the siege and instead attacked the island of Gozo. To commemorate this event (recorded in documents now in the Cathedral Museum, as well as by the historian Giacomo Bosio), a procession used to take place every year on the 5th February led by the Cathedral Chapter; also in thanksgiving, Don Giuseppe Manduca commissioned a painting of St. Agatha, a copy of which is now in this Chapel; the original (in the Cathedral Museum) was the altarpiece until 1694.

The Chapel was used to house two refugee families during the Second World War.

After the war, the Chapel of St. Agatha, an important part of the island's heritage, fell into disrepair. It was then that an appeal was launched and fund-raising commenced by the Mdina Cultural Association together with the Archbishop's Seminary (owners of the Chapel) which successfully restored the chapel.

# Cities and villages in Malta and Gozo

## Bahrija

### Bahrija: Malta's unspoilt countryside at its best

Baħrija is a small rural village in the limits of Rabat in the Western part of Malta. It has a population of around 3,000 that is gradually increasing with time. The name Baħrija translates to 'a moth' in English. There are two churches present, one of which is not used, and another one built in 1984, dedicated to Saint Martin of Tours, whose festa is celebrated on the 11th of November. During this day, several Maltese go along with the tradition and give a bag of mixed fruits and nuts to all children. An annual fair is held every Sunday following this feast, where a variety of goods are given away in a number of lotteries.

Located on high grounds, Baħrija is exposed to the cold winds coming from the north over the sea, and therefore has cooler weather than the rest of the island. There are panoramic views from this village, covering the north of Malta as well as the South West of Gozo, and if you're lucky, on days with good visibility, you can even see Sicily. In the southern side of Bahrija is the Qlejja Valley with its ridge having rock-cut water cisterns and silos dating from the Bronze Age (c. 1400 B.C.). These remains are a fairly steep climb up a rugged hill, but the hike is worth even for the views alone. The most important finds from this site are in the National Museum of Archaeology, Valletta.

Bahrija is well known for the beauty of its surrounding countryside, there are numerous walking treks. You can explore Fomm ir-Rih for a cliff walk, or explore the Victoria Lines starting from the Kuncizzjoni. There is also a farming community, growing mostly growing grape vines and other fruits that can withstand the harsh heat of summer and the high winds

## Things to do in Bahrija

### Bahrija country walk

**Take a walk around Bahrija and enjoy the fresh countryside air**

Bahrija country walk starts at the west side of Rabat, at the Nigret roundabout towards Fiddien, and is a long and beautiful walk that will take you through tranquil countryside, valleys surrounded by hills as well along breath-taking costal cliffs with views over the small natural reserve islet of Filfla. You will discover small farmhouses build in the cliff, old Roman excavations and maquis and pass through Bahrija - Bahrija Valley – Mtahleb – Tal-Vigarju Cliffs

After you leave the small village of Bahrija you will start your country walk towards Migra Ferha and walk further on to costal cliffs with amazing views. It is at this point that you can spot Filfla. As you continue walking, you pass by the remains of the Bronze Age village and several historical sites of interest. You will also spot the small and pretty Mtahleb church, built during the mid-17th century on the side of the cliff edge overlooking the ecologically protected Mtahleb Valley. As you keep walking you will arrive to Fiddien Valley to the northwest of Rabat and from there continue to the end of the walk in Rabat. Once you are back in Rabat you have several facilities such as restaurants, phone booths, health clinics and public transport.

The Bahrija country walk will take more or less 5 hours to complete and is 13 km long

# Dingli

## Dingli, majestic cliffs and the highest point of Malta

Dingli is a small village on the west coast of Malta, quite isolated from the rest of the villages. Dingli has a population of 3,326 persons living in an area of 5.7 km$^2$ and located on a plateau by the sea around 300 meters above sea level, on the highest point in Malta. Dingli cliffs fall straight down into the sea and provide open sea views over the small isle of Filfla.

Dingli has been inhabited since prehistoric time. Archaeologist date the town back to the times of the Phoenicians and the Carthaginians after some graves, dug out of the rocks, were found. The Romans who occupied Malta in 218 BC also used these same tombs. The village of Dingli most probably got its name from the surname of Maltese families who owned the land in the area. Today the inhabitants of Dingli make their living cultivating their fields for their own use but also selling some of the produce.

In Dingli one can find not only the breath taking Dingli cliffs but also Buskett Gardens, which is the only woodland area in Malta. Buskett Gardens is overlooked by Verdala Palace, which is the official summer residence of the President of Malta.

## Things to do and see inDingli

**Buskett Gardens:**

This is one of the greenest areas in Malta, Buskett Gardens houses many different type of trees, bushes and flowers. Buskett Garden is very popular for walks and picnics.

*Buskett provides a large green area with beautiful flowers and trees, a quiet space to relax in*

Buskett Garden is the only woodland area in Malta and is situated in the lush valley of Wied Il-Luq south of Rabat and east of Dingli.

Buskett Gardens was planted by the Knights of Malta to be used as a hunting ground. Today Buskett is one of the greenest areas in Malta: the gardens are also home to different type of trees such as orange, cactus, Mediterranean pines and cypress trees, bushes, shrubs and flowers. The garden also holds vineyards, olive and lemon groves.

Buskett Gardens can be explored by following the several peaceful pathways around the gardens and is a very popular place for picnics and nature lovers who want to discover the flora and fauna.

Buskett Garden is the greenest from autumn to spring with a lot of wild flowers and natural springs, however in summer the trees offer cooling shade from the hot sun.

In June, Buskett hosts the very popular L-Imnarja festival (the feast of St. Peter and St. Paul) with large crowds of visitors each year. The official residence of the President of Malta, the Verdala Palace is set on a hilltop overlooking Buskett Garden with more formal gardens. Verdala Palace has been the official summer residence of the President of Malta since 1987.

**Verdala Palace**

Verdala Palace has been the official summer residence of the President of Malta since 1987. The palace was built in 1586 by Grandmaster Hughes Loubenx De Verdalle is surrounded by Buskett Gardens, and a stone moat. The Place was used as a prison by Napoleon to be abandoned later on by the French. Governor Sir William Reid restored the Palace in 1858.

The Verdala Palace in Buskett is a beautiful piece of architecture that houses the summer residence of the President of Malta

The Verdala Palace is the official summer residence of the President of Malta. It was built by Grandmaster de Verdalle in 1586 on a site surrounding the woodland of Buskett, which was used by the Knights for game hunting.The Verdala Palace is surrounded by a stone ditch, and was embellished by several grandmasters over the years.The building is spread over two floors and at each corner, there are towers five storeys high.

During the French rule, the palace was used as a military prison and was largely abandoned after that. Verdala Palace was later restored by Sir William Reid in 1858 and it became the official summer residence of the British Governors.

The Verdala Palace has been the official summer residence of the President of Malta since 1987 and is generally closed to the public except for the annual Ball of the August moon held in aid of the Malta Community Chest Fund.

**Misrah Ghar il-Kbir** (Clapham Junction): These cart ruts date back to prehistoric times in Dingli, Malta. This is a network of tracks wooden cart wheels once dug in the rock.

**Dingli Cliffs**
The magnificient cliffs give spectacular sights when viewed from sea level or from top as they offer a wonderful view of the Mediterranean Sea and Filfla. The cliffs drop 250-300 meter into the sea with some flat slopes before dropping again to the sea. Local farmers have cultivated the slopes as small terrace fields. The cliffs stretch well beyond the village of Dingli.

Dwejra and The Azure Window, Gozo's pride
Concentration of natural monuments

Located on the West coast of Gozo, Dwejra is perhaps the most spectacular natural monument in Malta.

Geology, time, the elements and human intervention worked together to produce a fascinating area that features the Azure Window, an Inland sea, Fungus Rock, Dwejra bay, the Blue Hole, a watch tower and cart ruts.

Dwejra, which in Maltese means 'a small house', got its name from a tiny home built on the cliffs surrounding the inland sea.

The area has rare geological features both on land and underwater, rich and diverse wildlife and habitats and spectacular seascapes dominated by a rocky shoreline. There are some fascinating underwater caves and the nearby Blue Hole that provide excellent dive sites.

Overlooking the bay there is a chapel dedicated to St. Anne, built in 1963 on the site of a much older church. Dwejra is a tourist village that belonging to San Lawrenz for administrative purposes.

The Azure window

The Azure window is a natural arch that looks like a table over the sea. Two almost perpendicular vertical rocks hold a huge horizontal mass over them; a result of extensive fault-ins, as well as the wind and wave action on the rocks. It attracts a huge number of visitors and inspires many artists who paint the magical site on canvas.

It also featured in the movies “The Clash of the Titans” and “The Count of Monte Cristo”. The arch of the window is eroding with the actions of the wind and water; pieces of rock fall every now and then. It is expected that the arch will collapse sooner or later, so it is advisable not to walk on it.

The Inland sea

Known as ‘Il-Qawra’ by the locals, this area constitutes the lowest spot in Gozo. The Inland sea is an expanse of shallow water set in a deep recess in the coastline produced by the collapsing of underwater caves millions of years ago.

The bay is connected to the open Mediterranean Sea via a narrow 60 metre long tunnel in the cliffs, called Blue Cave because of the colour of the sea within it. There are small fishing boats that can take you from the inland sea, through the tunnel to the open sea withmajestic views of Fungus rock and the massive limestone cliffs.

Fungus Rock

The significance of Dwejra Bay is also due to a 65-metre high rock called Fungus Rock, known locally as 'Il-Gebla tal-General'. The name is derived from a commander of the Knights of St. John, who discovered a plant known as Malta Fungus or Cynomorium coccineum.

This rare parasitic flowering plant was highly prized by the Knights, since they believed it had medicinal properties and used it to dress wounds and as a cure for dysentery. Because of the importance of this plant, the Knights blocked access to the rock by smoothing the cliff sides, and placed a guarded it against intruders. There were tough punishments for trespassers or anyone caught stealing the crop.

Dwejra Coast Watch Tower

The Dwejra tower is situated just off the road that leads to Dwejra bay.

It was built during the reign of Grandmaster Antoine de Paule in 1651, with its main objective being to guard against attacks from the sea, but from 1744, it acquired another function, that of guarding Fungus rock and the plant that grew on it.

The tower lost its role as a coast guard in 1873 and was abandoned. In 1997, Din l-Art Helwa, started restoration works on the tower, and now it is open all year from Monday to Friday from 09:00 to 15:00, weekends and public holidays from 12:00 to 15:00.

The Cart Ruts of Dwejra

The couple of deep carved cart ruts in the Dwejra area ascend up the hill at the back of St. Anne's chapel to the soaring cliffs north of the Inland sea.

The purpose of these ruts is not known, and nobody knows what period of history they represent, but in any case, they are evidence of intense human activity during a particular era.

Apart from the cart ruts, pottery shreds found in the area evidence the presence of the first Neolithic culture of the Maltese Islands, some 7000 years ago.

The Flora around Dwejra

Although the Dwejra area is susceptible to human interference, agriculture and quarrying, it is nevertheless an important site with respect to its ecological value. There is a high level of biodiversity and endemism that was brought about by the Dwejra's relative isolation and inaccessibility. Species evolved to become endemic or rare.

Dwejra includes various habitats such as: steppe with a variety of grasses, garrigue areas hosting small bushes such as Tree Spurge (Euforbia dendroides), Golden Samphire (Inula crithmoided), and Maltese Salt Tree (Darniella melitensis), rocky shores with endemic sea lavenders, vertical cliffs hosting the Maltese Everlasting (Helichrysum melitense), as well as dry valley systems and freshwater wetlands.

Fauna & Birds flying over the Dwejra region
The Maltese Wall lizard is endemic to the Maltese and Pelagic Islands. There are five sub-species known, and the Dwejra area holds two distinct populations, with the Podarcis filfolensis generalensis confined just to Fungus rock. It is characterised by a dark reddish colour on the side, more prominent in males.

Dwejra is also a significant bird breeding and nesting site, especially on the high cliffs where it harbours several rare and endemic species. It is an ideal bird-watching spot particularly when winds from the North east and South east are blowing. The position and landscape of the site draw migratory birds that include wagtails, flycatchers and gulls. Other smaller birds such as the hirundines prefer moving along the coast on reaching the land when migrating. Groups of shorebirds can be seen at times battling against the wind to seek shelter provided by the coast. The cliffs offer good nesting spots for several birds including the Blue Rock Trush, Malta's National Bird.

The geology present in Dwejra

The geological features present in Dwejra are the result of marine erosion processes. The sea-cliffs are mainly composed of Lower Coralline Limestone, reaching a height of 130 metres. The almost perpendicular cliff face shows that the rock is very resistant to wave action.

The next layer Globigerina Limestone, is characterised by fossilised remains of sea creatures dating from the Miocene period. Slopes of Blue Clay can be seen in the Qawra valley that leads to the inland sea. When one sees an airline view of the Dwejra area, one can notice at least four circular structures imprinted in rock.

These features were underground caves whose roof collapsed during the Miocene period, forming hollow spaces or even sub-marine basins.

**St Mary Magdalena Chapel**: The chapel was dedicated to St Mary Magdalene and was built in 1646 by the nearby villagers. The chapel is located on the cliff top viewpoint south of Dingli. The chapel in Dingli has recently been restored with the construction date engraved above the entrance door

## Valletta

*Valletta, Malta's capital city and UNESCO World Heritage site*

Valletta has been built on a peninsula in the central eastern part of Malta and has a population of just over 6000 people. Valletta is named after the French Grandmaster Jean Parisot De La Valette who headed the defence of Malta from the Ottoman invasion in 1565. The entire city of Valletta has been declared a UNESCO World Heritage Site.

Valletta boasts many buildings from the 16th century, mostly baroque architecture that was built by the Knights of St. John. Amongst them is the majestic St. John's Cathedral, several auberges that hosted the

Knights in their times, the bastions surrounding the city, and several gardens. In fact, one could say that Valletta is actually a monument donated by the Knights.

Nowadays, Valletta hosts the National Parliament, the Law Courts, many Government Ministries and Departments, Administrative Offices, museums and plenty of shopping opportunities. The streets have a grid-like shape, so one could never really get lost while navigating through this open air museum.

The city is busy by day, but the Upper & Lower Barrakka Gardens offer a calm spot with incredible views of the Grand Harbour. Then as the sun sets, Valletta calms down and turns into a magic fortified city where the architecture stands out under the gentle lighting. Yet, with plenty of cafes, wine bars, theatres, exhibitions and other cultural events from time to time, Valletta is a living city all year long.

## Things to see and do in Valletta

Malta National Museum of Archaeology: This museum displays magnificent items from Malta's prehistory - including ornaments, pottery and tools.

Malta National War Museum: This museum represents the role that Malta had in the World Wars, presenting a collection of memorabilia from the war period.

Malta National Museum of Fine Arts: This museum has a sizeable collection of paintings and valuable local silverware, statues made of marble, bronze and wood, fine furniture objects and fine majolica pieces.

Malta Toy Museum: The toy museum displays an impressive collection of toys from the 1950's onwards.

Lascaris War Rooms: Visit Malta's most well-kept secret from World War Two.

Places of worship around Valletta

St. John's Co-Cathedral: St. John's Cathedral is a precious jewel from the 16th century located in the heart of Valletta. It was the religious seat for the

Knights of St. John, who enriched this place with the finest artefacts.

Anglican Cathedral of St. Paul: This Cathedral is one of the few Anglican sites present in Malta. Located in Independence Square, it rises above the skyline with a steeple 65 metres high.

Church of Our Lady of Victory: This small church was the first building to be constructed in Valletta after the Great Siege. It was the religious seat of the Knights until St. John's Cathedral was built.

Collegiate Parish Church of St. Paul's Shipwreck: This church is amongst the oldest and the most important churches in Malta, since it holds precious works of art as well as a relic from the spiritual father of the Maltese people, St. Paul.

Palaces and fortifications around Valletta

The Grandmaster's Palace & The State Rooms: This palace is located in the heart of Valletta and holds the

President's Office and the Parliament. It has splendid rooms and a fine armoury section.

The Palace Armoury: The Palace Armoury presents an impressive collection of armoury dating back to times of the Knights of St. John.

Casa Rocca Piccola: A privately owned home that offers an insight about the Maltese nobility over the last 400 years. It has over 50 rooms and a collection of furniture, silver artefacts and paintings.

St. James Cavalier: St. James Cavalier is a 16th century fort, which nowadays hosts a small theatre, a cinema, a cafe, music room and galleries.

Fort St. Elmo: Fort Saint Elmo is an important fortification that stands at the edge of Valletta; overseeing the entrances of both Marsamxett Harbour and the Grand Harbour.

Other interesting Valletta attractions

Manoel Theatre: The Manoel Theatre was constructed in 1731, but it's still in use today, holding a range of performances by various artists. The Manoel Theatre Museumportrays a powerful background of the fascinating history of the Manoel Theatre and the Royal Opera House that was destroyed during the Second World War.

National Library of Malta: Almost hidden by the cafes in Republic Square, the National Library of Malta (also known as Bibliotheca) is currently the legal deposit and copyright for Malta. The collection spans the personal libraries, thearchives and treasury manuscripts of the Knights of St. John, including archives from the medieval Università dei Giurati of Mdina and Valletta.

Hastings Gardens: Located on top of the bastions on the West side of the entrance to Valletta, the recently-embellished Hastings Gardens offer a magnificent view of the Marsamxett Harbour.

City Gate: The new Valletta City Gate, due to be completed by summer 2011, aims to give back the original expression to the city walls, enhancing their depth and strength while simultaneously opening up the view to Republic Street.

Victoria Gate: Victoria Gate is the main gate that leads from Valletta to the Grand Harbour. It substituted the quaint 'Porta del Monte' and was planned during the times of Sir Arthur Borton, who laid the foundation stone in 1884. Victoria gate was opened to the public in 1885. The wider arched entrances provided access to carriages, riders and vehicles, while pedestrians walked through the smaller doors on the sides. The arched entrances are decorated by Malta and Valletta's coats of arms while the top part is greatly decorated in the British style.

The Siege Bell Memorial: Overlooking the Great Harbour of Valletta, is the 10-ton bronze Siege Bell memorial that was unveiled by Queen Elizabeth and the President of Malta at the time, Dr. Censu Tabone, on the 29th May 1992, coinciding with the 50th anniversary from the award of the George Cross in 1942. The bell is mounted in a limestone tower, at the foot of which is a bronze figure representing the 7000 civilians and armed forces that died in Malta during the World War II between 1940 and 1943. The bell is rung daily, at noon.

The Law Courts: The Maltese Law Courts replace the Knights' Auberge d'Auvergne, built in 1570 and completely destroyed by a German parachute mine during World War II. The current building was built in the late sixties in a classical design. The Law Courts were inaugurated on the 9th of January, 1971 by the Prime Minister of the time Dr. George Borg Olivier and other distinguished guests. The first case to be heard at these Law Courts was scheduled for the 11th January, 1971 and was an appeal placed by two Sicilians in opposition to their extradition.

The Mediterranean Conference Centre: Adjacent to Fort St. Elmo and overlooking the Grand Harbour is one of the most impressive buildings of Valletta. The Mediterranean Conference Centre, which was used as a hospital for many years, is now used as a conference and exhibition space.

The Malta Experience: The Malta Experience is an audio-visual show covering 7,000 years of Malta's history. In 45 minutes, you will be taken on a journey to discover what happened since the early settlers first landed on the island, up until the recent history of the Second World War.

The Valletta Waterfront: The Valletta Waterfront is the gateway to Valletta if one is arriving by sea. More than half-a-million cruise passengers arrive annually in this attraction; that has impressive backdrop of the Grand harbour on one side and the elegant front and Valletta fortifications on the other side. The front has been recently renovated and now it offers an impressive number of facilities for cruise passengers and locals alike. There are a number of cafes, wine bars, alfresco dining, clubs, shopping possibilities, cultural and entertaining facilities, all set in colourful ancient warehouses that date back to the times of the Knights. From the Waterfront, you can take a bus, a taxi or a horse-drawn carriage to reach the centre of Valletta, and visit the rest of the city built by the Knights. Read more about getting to Valletta Waterfront!

## Mdina

### Mdina, Malta's silent city

Mdina is a fortified medieval town enclosed in bastions, located on a large hill in the centre of Malta. The town was the old capital of Malta, and with its narrow streets, few inhabitants and beatuful views over the Island it is truly a magical town. Mdina is referred to as the “Silent City” by Maltese and visitors alike - no cars (except those of a limited number of residents) have permission to enter Mdina and the town provides a relaxing atmosphere among the visitors walking its narrow streets and alleyways.

Mdina has a small population of around 250 people who live at 0.9km$^2$, within the city walls. In contrast, outside the city walls, the village of Rabat is just a step away, and has a population of over 11,000 people. The medieval town of Mdina presents a mix of Norman and Baroque architecture and is the home to many palaces, most of which today serve as private homes. The large and striking Cathedral of the Conversion of St. Paul stands in the main square of the town.

Mdina was first inhabited and fortified around 700 BC by the Phoenicians and was at that time called Maleth. Mdina benefits from its good location on the island's highest point, far away from the sea. Under the Roman Empire the Roman governor built his palace in Mdina and it is said that even St. Paul stayed there after he was shipwrecked in Malta.

It was the Normans who surrounded the city with its thick defensive fortificationsand they also widened the moat around Mdina. After an earthquake in 1693, there was the need to redesign parts of the city. This introduced Baroque designs within the city, and the Knights of Malta rebuilt the cathedral as well as the Magisterial Palace and Palazzo Falzon.

The gate that stands at the entrance today is not the original entrance; the bridge was built later on to enable cars and people to enter Mdina. The original entrance gate stands approximately 100 meters to the left.

## Things to do and see in Mdina

Natural History Museum: The Museum has an impressive collection with the reference collection holding over 10,000 rocks and minerals, over 3,500 birds, birds' eggs and nests, 200 mammals, over 200 fish species, thousands of local and exotic shells and insects.

Carmelite Church and Priory: This 17th century building offers visitors an opportunity to visit the spiritual way of life of the friars. The church and priory both have impressive works of art and are accompanied by a museum, gift shop and a cafeteria.

Palazzo Falzon: A well preserved medieval building which dates back to 1495. It holds an incredible collection of antiques.

St. Paul's Cathedral: This majestic Cathedral is located in the heart of Mdina, on the site where St. Paul converted Publius to Christianity. It is an artistic gem from the 17th century.

Cathedral Museum: Originally a seminary, the museum today is one of the most outstanding religious museums of Europe. It exhibits an impressive collection of sacred art, famous paintings, coin collections, Roman antiquities and original documents from the time of the Inquisition and the early Università. There is also a wonderful series of woodcarvings by Albrecht Durer, and much more.

Palazzo Santa Sophia: The basement of this house is assumed to be the oldest in siculo-norman style and dates back to 1233. The first floor, however, was added not earlier than 1938. All buildings that were erected between 1100 and 1530 are generally classified as "siculo-norman".

Torre dello Stendardo: This tower was constructed as a watchtower in 1750. On its roof a signal fire was set alight to warn the population in case of enemy attacks. It is now a police station.

Chapel of St. Agatha: This church was originally built in 1417, and redesigned by Lorenzo Gafà, in 1694. The church is dedicated to St. Agatha who, it is said, found shelter on Malta from the persecution of the Roman Emperor Decius (249 AD). Besides St Paul and St Publius, St Agatha is one of the three patron saints of Mdina.

Banca Giuratale: After Grandmaster Vilhena had confiscated the original Ministerial Palace for his own use, the Università found its new seat in this building. During the revolt against the French, a national assembly came together here. It elected a committee to consult with Lord Nelson, to get his assistance against the French. The Palazzo Giuratale became their headquarters.

Mdina Dungeons: The entrance is located inside the main entrance gate to Mdina, at the first turning on the right. Here, in the series of secret underground passageways, chambers and cells, a number of mysterious events from the dark side of Maltese history have been recreated.

Nunnery of St Benedict: The Benedictine nuns in Mdina are first mentioned in 1450. The present building is based on a medieval hospital for women. It was enlarged and totally restored in 1625.The rules of this Order are extremely strict, and the nuns are never allowed to leave the building, not even after their death. Every nun is buried in the crypt, and the only men allowed in are the doctor and the decorator. Today, about 20 nuns live there in total isolation, devoting their days to prayer and the maintenance of the garden.

Mdina Experience: This attraction provides a perfect start to a day in Mdina. Take a journey through timeand re-live the tragedies and triumphs brought to life before you in an audio-visual spectacular documentary that brings 3000 years of history alive. The Mdina Experience is found in a medieval building that is a museum in itself.

Visit Mdina after dark: Take a walk around the old Capital City of Mdina. Get to know the facts about important buildings, hear some fascinating tales and historical gossip. Mdina is the pivot of Malta's 7000 year history, and Prehistoric remains in the area can vouch for this. Go around the narrow, winding roads of medieval Mdina, while appreciating the baroque buildings the Knights have left us. Amazing views from the Belvedere shows off the beauty of Malta by night.

## Sliema

## Sliema, the Maltese hub for shopping, cafes and restaurants

Sliema is a coastal town situated on the northeast of Malta, adjacent to St. Julians. Once the home of Malta's aristocracy; it has now become a major commercial area, very popular for shopping, bars, cafes, restaurants and hotels.

Sliema acquired its name from a chapel dedicated to The Our Lady of The Sea (or Stella Maris) built in 1855, which served as a reference point to the fishermen who inhabited the area. The name is linked to the opening words of the Hail Mary prayer, which in Maltese are "Sliem Għalik Marija". Sliem is the Maltese word meaning peace or serenity. Sliema is quite a large residential town with a population of around 15,000 locals; housing also a significant number of expatriates that reside there temporarily.

Sliema was once a quiet fishing village, a minor summer resort that hosted the wealthier Valletta residents. The 19th century, however, saw the development of Sliema; it quickly grew into a residential area, adjoining to neighbouring St. Julians. Elegant villas and town houses, as well as many Victorian buildings were built by the British along the promenade overlooking the rocky coastline.

Soon, the people of Sliema understood the tourism potential of the area, and so they began a building boom that changed the whole landscape. Sliema became the first tourist resort in Malta, and its importance still remains. Nowadays, only a few Victorian and art nouveau houses remain, the rest have been replaced by modern apartment blocks, establishments and hotels.

From one side, the Sliema promontory offers spectacular views across to Valletta, and from the other side, there are breathtaking open sea views. The promenade that stretches for a couple of kilometres is ideal for long walks or runs, while the various benches provide a place for the locals to relax and socialize during warm summer evenings. Sliema coastline also boasts the Independence Garden completed with a children's playground, as well as two fortifications: a De Redin tower built in the 17th century to protect the islands against sea attacks; and another tower that was built by the British in a neo-gothic style in the 1880s.

**Sliema: Things to see and do**

Shopping: There a number of shopping opportunities in Sliema

Dine & Wine: Sliema is full of bars and restaurants, offering a wide variety of cuisines and atmospheres.

Take a walk at the promenade: To the right, the promenade leads you all the way to Gzira, Ta' Xbiex and Msida marina, while to the left, there's a walkway towards St. Julians, Paceville and St. George's Bay

## St. Julian's (San Giljan)

### St. Julian's, Malta's hub fore entertainment and nightlife

St. Julian's or San Giljan, is located on the Maltese coast, north of Valletta and it is mostly famous for its thriving nightlife and touristic activity. This town is a hub for new and luxurious hotels, many different kinds of restaurants and trendy nightclubs, mostly centred in an area known as Paceville.

For this reason, St. Julian's is popular amongst both the locals and tourists alike, especially during the summer months, where visitors take advantage of the good weather to enjoy long walks on the seafront promenade. The landscape of St. Julians is dominated by the tallest building in Malta, Portomaso Tower that stands at 98 metres.

St. Julian's has a population of around 8,000 people, and its name comes from the patron saint of the town, Saint Julian. The traditional summer festa is celebrated annually on the last Sunday of August.

Before 1800, St. Julian's was just a small fishing village surrounding Balluta and Spinola bays, with very few buildings except for the Spinola Palace, the old parish church, a few fishermen's huts and a few farm houses in the countryside. It appears that the St. Julian's area remained rural for so long because of the concern of attacks by the Muslims.

However, it seems that people dwelled in St. Julian's much earlier. In fact, in the 20th century, some tombs of the Roman period were discovered in Balluta, on the site where today there is the Chapel of the Sacred Heart Convent.

**St. Julian's: things to do and see**

Wine and Dine: There are a good number of bars and restaurants in St. Julian's offering a variety of cuisines and atmospheres.

Dance the night away in one of the numerous nightclubs around St. Julian's.

Balluta Bay: Balluta Bay is also popular amongst visitors; it is dominated by the neo-gothic church and the impeccaple Balluta Buildings built on the art nouveau style. There are also a couple of traditional terraced houses built in the Georgian-style.

Spinola Bay: Spinola Bay is one of the most romantic bays in Malta; going up the hill, one can admire the little old chapel, Spinola palace, a number of typical Maltese town houses decorated with traditional windows, as well as arched boat houses on the quay. During the evening, the street lights reflect on the calm sea that is full of quaint fishermen's boats.

Take a picture in the Love monument: This modern structure constructed out of Travertine was built with the intention that the word "LOVE" would be reflected in the calm waters of Spinola bay.

Go on a romantic boat trip: These 'love' boats take you and your loved one on a romantic cruise around Balluta bay. It's a perfect opportunity to capture the beauty of all the surroundings.

Spinola Palace: Spinola Palace was built in 1688, a building that is seen as the first stepping stone that started St. Julian's development. This palace and the adjacent gardens were built by Fra Paola Raffaele

Spinola "for the public entertainment" as written in the inscription found above the portico.

The palace was enlarged in 1733, however, during the French occupation, French troops made a mess of the place, damaging the emblem of the Knights that was on the façade.

Walk along the promenade: You can take a long walk on the promenade that stretches from St. Julian's all the way to Sliema, Gzira, Ta' Xbiex and Msida, and enjoy breathtaking views of the sea, Marsamxett harbour and Valletta. There are plenty of cafes, restaurants and bars along the way to keep you well fresh in the sunshine.

Visit Portomaso area: One of the poshest areas in Malta, Portomaso offers a number of shops with luxurious goods, high-class restaurants and a beautiful yacht marina.

## Birgu (Vittoriosa)

## Birgu, one of the Three Cities of Malta

Birgu, or Cittá Vittoriosa is one of the oldest city on the Island, and it played an important role in the Siege of Malta in 1565. 2,633 people inhabit the 0.5 $km^2$ city located on the south side of the Grand Harbour. Birgu was once a main city and has a long history of military and maritime activities.

Birgu's position in the Grand harbour was of great importance and several military leaders wanted to take over the city. Therefore, the Phoenicians, Greeks, Romans Byzantines, Arabs, Normans and the Aragonese all shaped and developed Birgu. Yet, no one did more for the city than the Knights of St. John, who arrived to Malta in 1530 and made Birgu the capital of Malta.

Birgu is a unique city surrounded by fortified walls, ancient history, monuments and places that one can visit. The entrance to Birgu is via the Couvre Porte, while the parish church is dedicated to St. Lawrence, whose feast is celebrated annually on the 10th of

August. Brass bands clubs, processions and fireworks are among the attractions in such festivities.

There is another church dedicated to Our Lady of the Annunciation and is run by the Dominican Order. It is also known as St. Dominic Church, and a smaller feast is celebrated every last Sunday of August.

**Birgu: Things to do and see**

The Parish Church: The parish church of St. Lawrence was the Conventual church of the Knights of St. John.

Inquisitor's Palace: The Inquisitor's Palace was the seat of the Inquisition in Malta from 1571 to 1798. The Palace has now been converted into a museum but before, it had its own chapel, library and rooms. However, once can still see the dungeons and the courtyard. The Museum is open every day and houses the national museum of ethnography collection.

Malta Maritime Museum: Exhibits maritime history from ancient to more recent times. The collections are unique and outstanding, especially those concerning the warships of the Knights of St John. There are also paintings, weapons, uniforms, anchors, maps and models dating from 1530 to 1798.

Notre Dame Gate: Grandmaster Fra Nicola Cotoner built this historical gate in Birgu in 1675. At the time it was built, it was the highest building in the region and from its terrace and roof there was an excellent view of a good part of the island. Today Notre Dame Gate houses the headquarters of Fondazzjoni Wirt Artna – the Malta Heritage Trust.

Malta at War Museum: The Museum holds an exciting exhibition about the II World War in Malta, with an underground air raid shelter. There is also a viewing of a 30-minute original wartime documentary. The museum exhibits a collection of wartime mementos, underground tunnels and audiovisuals. Open daily between 10:00 and 16:00.

Fort St. Angelo: After the Knights of Malta chose to settle in Birgu they made Fort St Angelo the seat of the

Grand Master. This is a historical piece of military architecture with its fortified walls. Some parts of the fort were leased to the Order of the Knights of St. John, forming an independent state over which Malta has no jurisdiction over. Other parts of the fort were trusted in the hands of Heritage Malta, who plan its restoration in the near future.

## Mellieha

### Mellieha, a picturesque town in the North of Malta

Mellieħa is a village located in the Northwest part of Malta. Mellieħa took its name from the ancient Punic and Roman salt-terms, as Mellieha means salt in Arabic. Mellieha is one of Malta's most attractive tourist and summer resorts with beautiful sandy beaches and blue sea. Mellieha has Malta's largest sandy beach, Għadira, which is perfect for families with small children, as the water remains shallow for a considerable distance from the shore. Mellieħa also has a lot of splendid seaside hotels, good restaurants and many traditional souvenir shops. During the summer months the population increases significantly due to many Maltese having summer residences in Mellieha, but the all year around inhabitants are around 7250 people in an area of 22.6 $km^2$.

According to archaeological discoveries, the town has been inhabited from Neolithic times to the Byzantine era, but the area was deserted after the Arab conquest. It was only during the time of the Knights, that Mellieha was once again inhabited. Mellieha was really developed under the British colonization who gave leases to encourage people to settle. Today Mellieha is still popular with foreign house buyers. The people of Mellieha are famous for their friendliness and hospitality and most people who visit Mellieha feel welcomed and at home.

Mellieha's main Village Feast "Il-Vitorja" is held in the beginning of September and it reaches its peak on 8th September. During this popular feast, the village is full of activities such as musical concerts, fireworks, folk singing, food stands, and exhibitions and of course many religious processions in honour of Our Lady of Victories. The Mellieha village feast is a great experience to both tourists and locals.

For tourists choosing to spend their holiday in Mellieha it is worth renting a car, as it is about 20/30 minutes from St Julian's.

**Mellieha: Things to do and see**

Ghadira Bay: Easily accessible, this spot is a favourite with families, who tend to stay out for the day. There are sun beds and umbrellas for rent, but there is still space on this wide beach for anyone wishing to bring their own equipment. There are plenty of snack bars and small cafes and the beach offers different types of water fun, such as pedal boats rental, parasailing or large floating play areas.

Ghadira Natural Reserve: The nature reserve encloses two types of habitat that are very rare in Malta: wetland and salt marsh. The area was declared a bird sanctuary in 1978 after BirdLife Malta presented scientific data to the government showing the ornithological value of the wetland (read more here).

Armier Bay: The sandy beach at Armier stretches around the shore of an open bay and is just a short drive away from Ghadira bay. This sandy bay has a lovely view over the Islands of Comino and Gozo. Bars and small restaurants provide the necessary beach facilities.

Popeye's Village: This popular attraction is the film set of the 1980 film, Popeye. Popeye's Village has daily shows for the tourist as well as rides for the younger children, slides, trampolines and a Lido.

St. Agatha's Tower: This Tower, guarding the bays of Mellieha and Ghajn Tuffieha, is more known as the Red Tower. It was built to act as a signalling post in 1647 for communication with the island of Gozo, so it's natural that it dominates the skyline of Malta's Marfa Ridge. It originally housed cannon, 30 men and enough food to withstand a siege for 40 days (read more here).

White Tower Bay: White Tower Bay is enclosed by a fortification wall that was built by the knights.

# Bugibba

## Bugibba, a seaside tourist resort with a buzzing nightlife

Bugibba is located in the North East part of Malta; it is one of Malta's largest seaside villages with a numerous hotels, restaurants, clubs and pubs. Bugibba has a seaside promenade stretching from Salina Bay to St Paul's Bay, very popular amongst thetourists and locals alike. The promenade offers beautiful views of the open sea and St. Paul's Island. The coastline is a bit rocky, but these are flat rocks, providing a good place for sunbathing and swimming. Bugibba's many playgrounds and wide variety of entertainment options makes it popular with families. The city's lively nightlife readily entertains adults with cinemas, bingo halls, karaoke bars and even a casino.

Bugibba has been developed into a seaside resort with many hotels and holiday apartments along the coastline. It is the favoured summer residence of many, including the President Emeritus of Malta.

**Bugibba: things to see and do:**

Scuba diving: Go scuba diving with any of the diving centres available in Bugibba. Throughout the courses & dive expeditions their instructors ensure that all your dives are memorable.

The Oracle Casino: The casino located in Bugibba, Malta, opened its doors to the public in 1998. Internationally trained, multi-lingual staff is there to ensure the guests enjoy gaming in a friendly and professional environment.

There is a megalithic temple in the centre of town that is worth visiting. It has a large hotel built around it. Access can be gained through the hotel or casino lobby (feel free to ask the staff for directions if necessary). The hotel is located on the sea front in the middle of the block between Triq Il-Merluzz and Triq Ghawdex and access is easiest from the rear of the building.

## Qawra

### Qawra: A popular seaside and tourist resort

Qawra is a seaside resort located on the North part of Malta, very close to Bugibba, and St. Paul's Bay. The town was built with the purpose of attracting British tourists, and in fact, it is constellated of hotels, holiday apartments, restaurants, cafes shops, bars, casinos, and many other tourist facilities. Water sports dominate the shoreline, and although there are no sandy beaches, swimming, sunbathing and diving are still very popular activities.

There is a long promenade that stretches for around 3km all the way to St. Paul's Bay. This walkway outlines the rocky shoreline, and provides fantastic views of the open sea. It offers a perfect space for leisurely walks and jogs, especially during the evenings, where the sunset colours the sky with spectacular hues.

There were some Neolithic remains found in Qawra, which are now incorporated in the landscaped grounds of the Dolmen hotel.

Qawra is also the site of one of the many towers built by the Knights in 1637. Standing on Qawra point, this small watch tower watches St. Paul's Bay to the West and Salina Bay to the east. The tower is now used as a restaurant, however additions to the building took away its authenticity.

**Qawra: Things to see and do**

Visit the parish church: The parish church of Qawra is a recent construction by Richard England; in fact, it was inaugurated as a parish on the 8th of December, 2004. It is dedicated to St. Francis of Assisi, whose feast is celebrated annually on the 17th of September.

Visit the Malta Classic Car Museum: Enjoy a great trip down to memory lane with a great collection of classic automobiles dating back to the golden age.

Dive or try any of the watersports available in the area.

Swim and sunbathe along the rocky shoreline.

Take a walk or jog along the seaside promenade

## Marsaxlokk

### Marsaxlokk, fishing village constellated with colourful luzzus

Marsaxlokk village is located in the south-eastern part of Malta which is famous for its big Sunday fish market and its many decorative "eyed" painted boats called Luzzus. The village has around 3200 inhabitants and in the past, most of the inhabitants worked as fishermen. The name Marsaxlokk comes from the word "marsa" which means port and the word "xlokk" which means south in Maltese.

Marsaxlokk has an old history dating back to the ninth century BC. It was in this bay that the first Phoenicians arriving in Malta landed and set up their businesses. It was here that the Turkish fleet anchored during the Great Siege in Malta.  Marsaxlokk's hill of Tas-Silg was used as a religious site and still contains remains of megalithic temples of the Tarxien phase. There were also Bronze Age tools found on the hill.

Even though Marsaxlokk is a charming village with its traditional, brightly painted Luzzus, tasty fish restaurants and its green water, tourists at times don't visit the town due to its shipyards and power station. Malta's main power station is located here and Oiltanking Malta Ltd. also operates from Marsaxlokk. The Malta Freeport in Marsaxlokk terminal has developed over the years and is now one of the largest container terminals in the Mediterranean.

Marsaxlokk has a small sandy beach on the east side, and stunning St. Peter's Poolat Delimara is 20 min away by foot. St. Paul's bay is excellent for diving, snorkelling and cliff jumping down into the natural pool. The smooth, weathered limestone ledges make good sunbathing spots at St. Peters Pool. Don't miss the saltpans that can be seen at this location either.

**Marsaxlokk: Things to do and see**

St Peters Pool: This stunning rocky part of the shore provides a quiet spot for swimming and sunbathing.

Parish Church: Marsaxlokk church is dedicated to Our Lady of the Rosary, The Madonna of Pompeii. There are various village feasts with religious processions and spectacular firework displays in honour of Our Lady on the 8th of May, 1st Sunday in August, and 1st Sunday in October. Inside the church one can see the statue of the Madonna and Child, which came from Lecce, Italy in 1900.

The Fish Market: The popular fish marked attracts hundres of locals and tourists who are interested in buying the freshest catch.

Luzzus: These colourful boats provide a spectacular scene in Marsaxlokk Bay

# Victoria (Rabat)

## Victoria and the Citadel, Gozo's new and old capital cities

Victoria is the capital city of Gozo, also known among the Maltese as Rabat. It includes both the old Rabat town and the Citadel – the antique city on top of the hill. In fact, Rabat means 'suburb' in Arabic, meaning that the town was a suburb of the Citadel. The town has a population of around 7,000, making it the most populated town in Gozo. The name Victoria was given in 1887 in honour of the famous British Queen's Golden Jubilee celebrations, and the town was also raised to a city status.

The Cittadella is located on a hill, in the geographical nucleus of the island, and has been called, appropriately, the Crown of Gozo. It seems that the Citadel had already been the centre of since prehistoric times, around 7000 years ago. However, it was first fortified during the Bronze Age approximately around 1500 BC, further developed by the Phoenicians and finalized into an Acropolis during the Roman Times. The massive defensive stone walls rising above the town were constructed by the Knights to shelter the villagers from attacks. There are many attractions in Victoria and a visit to the Citadel is a must.

The centre of Rabat is Independence Square, also known as it-Tokk, dominated by the Banca Giuratale, built between 1733 and 1738. This building was the seat of the municipal government of Gozo, while nowadays it hosts the Victoria Local Council. The square is buzzing with activity in the morning; a daily open-air market sells all sorts of tourist souvenirs, while a number of cafes surround the square, offering cold beverages and pastizzi to the visitors.

The Grand Basilica dedicated to St. George is in the centre of the old town, just off Independence Square. The small streets surrounding the basilica are the oldest in town and are worth a walk around; you'll be impressed by the local delicacies sold in the small shops.

The main road, Republic Street, is the commercial heart of the city. A couple of shopping arcades, banks, band clubs and opera theatres dominate this street, while you can also find Villa Rundle Public Gardens for a relaxing time away from the noise of the city

**Victoria: Things to see and do**

Visit the Citadel: From this fortified city, you can enjoy fantastic views of the whole of Gozo. Within the Citadel, you can find the Gozo Cathedral – a fine 17th century baroque building that is famous for its outstanding trompe l'oeil painting depicting a dome that was never there. You can also find the Cathedral Museum, the Law Courts, the Old Prison, the Gozo Museum of Archaeology, The Folklore Museum, the Citadel Armoury, and the Natural Science Museum. From time to time, there are art exhibitions in different areas of the citadel, ranging from paintings, photography and artistic fashion jewellery amongst others.

Villa Rundle: Villa Rundle public gardens were opened by the British in 1910. These gardens provide a space of calm and relaxation away from the noise and traffic of the town. These gardens are situated between Republic Street and the Main Car Park in Victoria. One can see in a bronze bust of the Gozitan 18th century historian and grammarian Can. Gian Pietro Agius de Soldanis and another of Gozo born French poet and writer Laurent Ropa.

Visit the shopping centres Arkadia and The Duke for some fashion shopping.

Take a walk around the old streets of Rabat and visit St. George's Basilica and the open-air market in Independence Square

# Culture of Malta explained

## A mixture of societies of cultures over long centuries

The culture of Malta is the result of the many different societies that came in contact with the Maltese Islands throughout history, including cultures of neighbouring countries, cultures of nations that ruled Malta for long centuries, and other influences from tourism and media.

The culture of modern Malta is a rich one, composed of traditions, beliefs and practices that resulted out of a long process of adaptation and assimilation of different societies over time. Subjected to these historic processes, the Maltese culture also incorporated the linguistic and ethnic admixture that defines who the Maltese people are.

The Maltese culture of today can be effectively defined as being Latin European with influences from the British period of history quite evident. Arab influences are very apparent in the Maltese language and perhaps a bit in the Mediterranean diet, but they're not seen anywhere else. Latin European influences remain predominant mainly because of the island's rulers in the past eight centuries as well as the fact that Malta shares religious beliefs and many traditions with its Sicilian and Southern European neighbors.

**Semitic influence**

Malta was inhabited by the Phoenicians from around 700 BC who exploited the shelter of Malta's harbours. By 480BC, as Carthage was growing its empire in the Western Mediterranean, Malta became a Punic colony. Exposure to semitic influences continued to an during the 268-year rule of the Knights of St. John, in part because of trade, but mainly because of the large numbers of slaves present in Malta during the 17th and 18th centuries.

Dramatic incidents related to piracy and slavery remain with us till today, reflected in Maltese folklore, superstitions, beliefs, sayings and in the Maltese literature, with works such as Inez Farrug written by Anton Manwel Caruana in 1889 (1889) and the traditional ballad of l-Gharusa tal-Mosta, which narrates the kidnap of a Maltese bride by Turkish pirates.

**Influences of Catholicism on Maltese culture**

It is said that in Malta, Gozo, and Comino there are around 365 churches; or one church for every day of the year. Every town has its parish church as the focal point and a main source of civic pride. This pride is beautifully manifested during festas; celebrating the day of the patron saint of each parish with marching bands, processions, fireworks and other festivities.

According to tradition, and as recorded in the Acts of the Apostles, the Church in Malta was founded by St. Paul in 60AD, following his shipwreck on these Islands. The earliest Christian place of worship in Malta is known to be St. Paul's Grotto – the place where St. Paul was imprisoned during his stay on Malta. Evidence of Christian practices and beliefs during Roman persecution can be found in the many catacombs that lie underground around Malta. There are also a number of cave churches, including the grotto at Mellieħa, where St. Luke is said to have painted a picture of the Madonna.

Under the rulings of the Norman, Spanish and the Knights, Malta became the devout Catholic nation it is today. It is worth noting that the Inquisition had a very long history in Malta – established by the Pope in 1530, with the last Inquisitor departed in 1798, after the Knights surrendered to the forces of Napoleon Bonaparte.

**Influences of migration**

Malta's position as a maritime nation paved the way for extensive interaction between Maltese seamen and their colleagues around the Mediterranean. Moreover, by the mid-19th century, the Maltese had already a history of migrating to other places, including Egypt, Greece, Sicily and other islands in the Mediterranean. Intermarriages where quite common, while migrants would return to Malta from time to time, importing new customs and traditions that been absorbed into mainstream Maltese culture as time went by.

Migration was heavy once again after World War II, where around a third of the Maltese population left to start a new life in faraway lands, namely Australia, Canada, UK and US. In the 1990s many Maltese and second generation migrants returned to Malta. Recent years have seen an increase in the number of foreign expatriates moving to Malta, creating an increasingly cosmopolitan environment in the towns and around Malta.

**A few basics of the Maltese culture:**

- ✓ The Maltese culture is a combination that comes alive by different societies that interacted with the Maltese people over time. Read about how the Maltese culture was influenced by each ruler in the history of Malta.
- ✓ The Maltese are a very devout Catholic nation, and religion still has an important place in the

modern Maltese society. Read about Religion in Malta

- ✓ Maltese people spend a lot of time and energy discussing politics. Especially

# Weather and climate in Malta and Gozo

**Maltese climate**

The climate in Malta is a Subtropical Mediterranean one, with long, hot, dry and very sunny summers and short, mild and slightly rainy winters. This kind of climate is typical of most of the counties in the Mediterranean Basin. The weather in Malta is stable and the average temperature is 22-23°C during the day whilst during the night it is 15°C.

The sea temperature is 20°C during January and 26°C in August. Swimming is therefore possible all year round (for the hardier people) with the sea temperature rarely dropping below 15°C. From June to November, the average sea temperature exceeds 21 °C.

## Rainfall and sunshine in Malta

Malta is one of the countries with the highest number of sunshine hours per year in Europe, double of many cities in the north of the region. Malta has an average of more than 5 hours of sunshine per day in December to over 12 hours of sunshine in July adding up to around 3,000 hours of sunshine a year. To compare, London only has 1,461 hours of sunshine a year.

The annual rainfall in Malta is low, averaging 578mm a year, and during the summer months there can be very long dry spells without a drop of rain. Almost three-fourths of the yearly rainfall falls between October and March. Malta has strong winds and the most common are the cool north-westerly winds and the dry north-easterly winds. There is also the very hot and humid south-easterly wind. Humidity in Malta is a problem for some as it is always relatively high and rarely falls below 40%.

## Summers in Malta

Summers in Malta are hot, dry and very sunny with August usually the warmest month. In August temperatures in Malta vary from 28-34°C during the day and cool down to 19-24°C during the night a. The summer season lasts 8 months and the weather start warming up in April, with a temperature of 19-23°C during the day and ends in November with temperatures of 17- 25°C during the day. However, it is not unusual that the temperature reaches 20° C during the day in the remaining four months. Due to the high humidity percentage in Malta, it can become quite unbearable to stay in the sun during the summer months, especially during August and September. On the other hand, the sea breezes are cooling in summer especially along the coasts and beaches where its ideal to spend your day.

**Winters in Malta**

Winters in Malta are usually mild. The coldest month is January with temperatures ranging from 12-20°C during the day and 7-15°C during the night. When the weather cools down it is due to the North winds from central Europe. During the winter, which lasts from December to March, the daytime temperature hardly ever drops below 10°C. Malta has the warmest winters in Europe, with an average temperature of 15-16°C during the day that drops to 9-10°C during the night. Snow does not fall in Malta, but during the winter months it tends to get pretty windy from wind blowing from the northeast. These winds usually last around three days. Thunderstorms make up most of the rainfall during the winter months.

## Average weather data for the Maltese Islands

| MONTH | Temperature | Rainfall | Sunshine | Humidity |
|---|---|---|---|---|
| January | 14°C (57F) | 90mm | 6 hours | 67% |
| February | 15°C (59F) | 60mm | 7 hours | 66% |
| March | 17°C (62F) | 39mm | 8 hours | 65% |
| April | 19°C (66F) | 15mm | 9 hours | 64% |
| May | 23°C (73F) | 12mm | 10 hours | 63% |
| June | 26°C (79F) | 2mm | 12 hours | 60% |
| July | 30°C (86F) | 0mm | 12 hours | 59% |
| August | 31°C (88F) | 8mm | 12 hours | 62% |
| September | 28°C (82F) | 29mm | 8 hours | 64% |

| | | | | |
|---|---|---|---|---|
| October | 24°C (75F) | 63mm | 7 hours | 65% |
| November | 20°C (68F) | 91mm | 6 hours | 67% |
| December | 17°C (62F) | 110mm | 5 hours | 68% |

# The End